Shoo-Fly
and
Other Folk Tales From Upstate

By Donald J. Sawyer

THEY CAME TO SACANDAGA, THE STORY OF GODFREY SHEW: FISH HOUSE PATRIOT

Shoo-Fly
and
Other Folk Tales From Upstate

by
Donald J. Sawyer

Illustrations and Cover by
Walter Jerome

MAYFIELD BOOKS
Gloversville, New York—12078

Library of Congress
Catalog Card Number: 84–61376
ISBN 0–9613682–0–9

Printed by
THE BARONET LITHO COMPANY, INC.
Johnstown, New York
1984

To Dean, my wife, for her encouragement and help during the getting together of these stories.

Contents

viii

Introduction

The stories and anecdotes in this collection have been related to me by folk living in the Adirondack foothills and uplands of the Mohawk Valley. Most of them came from people in the Fulton County area of upstate New York where I was born and have always lived. To reach this "off the beaten path" one must leave the highly traveled New York Thruway (exit 27 or 28) and journey northward toward the foothills of the Adirondack Mountains. There are two small cities in the county—Johnstown, which is the county seat, and Gloversville. Villages and hamlets are scattered, hit or miss, about the rolling countryside and include Broadalbin, Vail Mills, Fish House, Mayfield, Northville, Rockwood, Perth, Meco and others.

Folklore sidetracked me from my real estate business. The location of my office might have had something to do with it; not right in the heart of Gloversville businesss district, but far enough up

North Main Street where people feel they can wander in and stay awhile. The old general store has been replaced by the super market and people miss the cracker barrel. So I guess that's one of the reasons they came into my office. Also, I'm a good listener and not above swapping a tale or two.

According to those who told me the stories, many are about people who actually lived, and places which exist even today. An exception being the lands flooded to make way for the Sacandaga Reservoir (now called Great Sacandaga Lake). Small settlements, portions of villages and a vast vlaie were inundated. But even under water these places resurface in our folk stories to bring alive that unforgettable past.

B. A. Botkin, eminent folklorist wrote, "The good folk story teller is not simply a transmitter. He is also a creator with a native story sense and a feeling for the authentic, expressive detail, the right phrase, and the lively image, plus a good memory and an insight born of identification with the people who are his neighbors, his kinfolk, and his forebears."[1]

1. Taken from *A Treasury of New England Folklore* by B. A. Botkin. Copyright © 1965 by B. A. Botkin. Used by permission of Crown Publishers, Inc.

I hope the reader will find some of the attributes listed by Mr. Botkin at work in this group of stories. Resource material for many of the stories and anecdotes, and sometimes further development of the story, can be found under the individual title in the Appendix.

D. J. S.

Gloversville, N. Y.

Acknowledgments

Grateful acknowledgment is made for permission
to reprint the following stories written by the author:

NEW YORK FOLKLORE QUARTERLY

The Story of Bull Run
Nickname
The Dominie
A Church From Devil's Money
Shoo-Fly

NEW YORK FOLKLORE

Sleigh Ride For A Corpse

ASIA CALLING

The Amah's Prayer

The Story of Bull Run

How does it happen there is a place in Fulton County called Bull Run? For almost thirty years I have tried, without success, to find the answer. Whenever I ask a native living in the area, we both agree that the famous battle of Bull Run was fought in Virginia. No one knows of any battle ever being waged in the seemingly sleepy little settlement nestled at the base of Bleecker Mountain in the Adirondacks.

Then one day my work as a real estate broker took me to the home of a young couple to whom I was selling a house. They had obtained the help of the wife's mother to stay with their children while we went downtown to close the realty trans-action. I was properly introduced to the mother and somehow during our ensuing conversation it became apparent that she had come from the section called Bull Run.

"You did!" I exclaimed. I hardly dared expect

the sought for answer. But hope began to burn anew. "How did it ever happen to be called that?"

In a very matter-of-fact way she said, "I can tell you."

How could she be so calm, possessing such knowledge? Little did she realize that I was as excited as if I had actually discovered the pot of gold at the end of the rainbow! "Yes?" I said impatiently.

"You see, my ancestors were among the first to settle in that region. I can remember my grandfather, when a very old man, telling me the story.

"There was a family named Bull who lived across the road from my grandfather. Mr. Bull, who was not an overly ambitious man, had a habit of coming home almost every Saturday night in a 'tipsy' condition. On one particular Saturday he could hardly make it up the path to the front door of his house.

"It was a warm moonlit night and my grandfather had come out on the porch with a friend, who was leaving to go home. They had enjoyed the evening playing Pitch and stood there visiting for a minute or two when they saw Mr. Bull walking rather unsteadily up the road. They continued to watch the dramatic events which followed.

"Mr. Bull weaved his way up the path to his home and pounded upon the front door, calling for

2

his wife to let him in. Mrs. Bull threw open the door, illuminating them both in a shaft of yellow lamp light. She had a long-handled broom raised over her head and brought it down with a solid 'whack' upon Mr. Bull. This seemed to sober him up almost immediately, and turning on his heel he ran down the path toward the open road, his wife in close pursuit.

"My grandfather's companion laughingly yelled, 'By golly, look at old Bull run!'

"This episode was told and re-told those many years ago and gradually the area became known to all in the surrounding territory as the place where Bull run. Then finally just 'Bull Run.'"

See Appendix: The Story of Bull Run.

The Dominie

Dominie Clemans was no ordinary man of the cloth, as those farm folk who lived in Fulton County would tell you. From the very first rumblings of a civil war between the States, he voiced his views loud and clear from the pulpit. He was against slavery, and if war did come he would leave the ministry and join the army.

The Dominie was as good as his word, and shortly after war had been declared he gave notice to his congregation to find another preacher for their church. "But I'll be back," he assured them.

The people loved the Dominie and gave him a splendid farewell party. After that, almost four years went by and no one heard from him. Some rumored he had been killed, while others reasoned he probably found a place he liked better than Fulton County. Then one Fall day in 1864, a man, dressed in Union Soldier's uniform, came walking up the dirt road toward the little white church. His short, stocky build and a certain spring in his walk left no doubt that Dominie Clemans had come back.

The people were joyous and the church was filled to overflowing the first Sunday after his return. His dark hair glistened with a few grey hairs which hadn't been there when he left, and his brown eyes, always expressive, seemed deeper with understanding. His voice still had a quality which stirred you all up inside and started you thinking about something more than the price for new potatoes or how much butter and eggs were bringing at the store.

One February, several Sundays after the Dominie's return, not many of the congregation were in church. And no wonder. It had snowed for two days and nights. Then the wind had gathered up the buoyant, freshly fallen flakes, swirling the countryside into a land of mountainous white dunes.

An elder, whose job it was to start a fire in the big iron stove early each Sunday during the winter, had been late that morning. It was still cold in the church when service started. For this reason the sermon was shorter than usual. Immediately after it was over, and they had sung a hymn, the Dominie descended from his pulpit, walking up the aisle to the door to shake hands with those few who had braved the weather.

One of the men said, while shaking hands with the Dominie, "You didn't have much of a message this morning."

The Dominie looked at the man, then at the few people who had come to church, and said, "What would you have me do, load a cannon to shoot a chipmunk!"

There were many stories the Dominie told about his experience while soldiering with the Grand Army of the Republic. One that has remained alive over the years is about his first tour of guard duty.

The Company had been traveling all day in the rain, and the captain decided to make camp near a large farm they were approaching. Here was food and water and the men would have a chance to dry out. They were soaked to the skin and their boots caked with mud.

After camp had been made, Private Clemans drew guard duty and now stood outside the captain's tent. They were bivouacked on a rise of ground back of a large barn. From here could be seen much of the woods and field.

"Clemans, I'll get someone to relieve you here. I want you to go down and guard the farmer's hay by the barn. The men might get ideas about it," said the captain, nodding toward the hay.

"Yes, sir," said Private Clemans, saluting smartly. Then, turning right-face he walked down the hill toward the large haystack. He hadn't been there long when a soldier walked over to him and said, "The ground is so dang wet and cold from all the rain. How about some hay to sleep on tonight?"

Private Clemans knew what the soldier was talking about. It would be much more comfortable to bed down with a dry pallet. Suddenly, with a wave of compassion, he said: "You're not allowed to take any of this hay. Captain's orders. But I'm going to walk around and take a look at the other side of the pile." And so saying, he walked away from the soldier.

In the army, news travels like greased lightning—be it true or false. In a few minutes another soldier came asking for hay. And again Clemans looked the other way. This happened more times than one dare count, until what was once a plump mound of hay, now looked sadly deflated.

The following morning when the captain discovered what had happened, he was furious. "What is this?" he bellowed. "Who took the hay, Clemans?"

"I didn't see anyone take it," replied Clemans. And he hadn't.

"Then what you need is more experience as a guard. I'm placing your name permanently on the guard roster. That's what you need, more experience," said the captain with some degree of satisfaction.

It would be difficult to determine who was more enraged—the captain or the farmer. The farmer received some restitution when he was given a sum of money collected from the men in the company.

"Worth it," said one of the soldiers. "Best sleep I've had in weeks!"

Private Clemans had almost uninterrupted guard duty. Other men would have cried for mercy. He walked with a slump and his eyes were red-rimmed from lack of sleep. Finally, even the captain took pity and had Clemans' sentence rescinded.

The "guard duty" story was a favorite with the parisioners. Some Sundays, when the Dominie stood in the pulpit to warn and reprimand, and reminding them of the wages of sin, they would think about that pile of hay, smile to themselves, and feel more comfortable.

See Appendix: The Dominie.

More Stories About the Dominie

The Dominie had always been a lover of fine horses and always had one. Everyone knew that. And now that he was home again it didn't take him long to acquire as dandy a three year old sorrel stallion as you ever laid eyes on. He usually drove a three-quarter buggy with the open Bible on the seat beside him. There were several small churches in his area and it gave him much satisfaction to have a good horse for traveling from one country church to another. And too, his people for the most part lived on farms and were separated by some distance. When an emergency came up or there was a shut-in, they expected him.

But his obvious worldly pride in the ownershp of such a fine horse was of growing concern to his parishoners. They finally delegated one of the church trustees to talk with him about it.

Clyde Hastings had that opportunity just a few days later when the Dominie was driving past his farm and slowed down to say hello. He walked over to the buggy and after some hemming and hawing said, "Dominie, don't you think this horse is a little too good for the preacher to be driving?"

Dominie Clemans peered at the man for a moment, then brought his hand down with a thump on the Bible beside him. "Sir, nothing is too good to carry the word of God. Giddap!" and off he took, with all the speed of which the horse was capable.

* * * * * * * *

A few weeks after the incident with Clyde Hastings, on a Sunday morning in June, the Dominie entered a chapel near North Broadalbin. The church had too small a membership to afford a steady preacher, so the various ministers in the area and lay people too, took turns filling the pulpit.

This morning the Dominie had an especially good sermon prepared and was looking forward to speaking to the limited but usually attentive audience. However, there was someone else, a young man,

12

who had arrived ahead of him and also expected to preach.

"Who," inquired the Dominie, "sent you?"

"Why, the presiding elder," said the young man, his face reddening slightly under the intense glare of the older preacher.

"Then," said the Dominie, "You go back and tell him that Jesus Christ sent me. I am going to preach."

And he did.

Sleigh Ride for a Corpse

I feel like a traitor to my class, but it all happened quite innocently. An attorney who is also a friend of mine said he needed a professional real estate appraisal and asked if I would help him out. "Sure," I replied. "Fill me in on the details and I'll take care of it for you." The conversation was via telephone. "Let's get together this coming Saturday morning if the weather is good," said the attorney. "I'll stop for you; the property is just outside Gloversville, the Calldwin farm. No need of us going in separate cars." I agreed to his plan.

Saturday morning dawned grey and damp but true to typical Fall weather, it burned off by the time he drew up in front of my house at 10 A.M. On the way to the farm the lawyer explained the situation. "Mr. Calldwin has been offered a good sum for allowing the gas and electric company to install a power line across a portion of his farm.

15

He was satisfied, but then he discussed it with his attorney and now they are suing for a larger settlement. Of course, I represent the power company," he said.

I felt uneasy. Maybe they were offering him a big cash settlement for the land they were using, but it was Calldwin's farm and he might not like those stoical giants striding across his pastures and through his woods.

When we arrived and I inspected the property, I was torn by two thoughts: much of the land was stony and hilly where the poles had been placed, and the amount of money the power company had offered seemed fair enough from the standpoint of economics. But there was more. The farmer would never again be able to arise in the morning, go out on his porch and look across his land without seeing a trespasser. He would always experience a jolt when he saw the power poles. They had invaded his right to privacy and marred a scene he cherished more with each passing year.

But I was hooked. I'd given my word to do the job, and went back to the farm several times. It took many hours of walking over the land, studying values of adjoining properties, neighborhood trends, comparable sales and borings of the soil. It is customary for two real estate appraisers to make separate appraisals in cases like this. I give my lawyer friend credit; he located a very capable man, Mr. Thompson, who had been an appraiser of farm and rural property for many years. Mr. Thompson also owned and lived on his own farm near Salisbury Center.

During the hours Mr. Thompson and I spent together, we had time to talk of things other than the appraisal and the hearing of the case before the commissioner. One day during the proceedings we went out for lunch recess. We talked of farming, his farm in particular, and then we told a few stories. When he learned I collected folklore he said, "I'll tell you one that happened over my way."

The following is the story Mr. Thompson told to me: Over near Oppenheim in Fulton County, at a place called Middle Sprite, there's an old saltbox farmhouse. If you drive past it during the summer months and see the gnarled sugar maples in front of the place and the large weeping willow standing there in the side yard like a shaggy sheep dog, you'd never guess the hill rising rather abruptly in back of the house was the scene of a weird winter sleighing party.

Tim O'Brien was dead in the middle of the

winter. The snow was piled high along the road in front of the house and along the drive leading to the woodshed and barn. The routine of the little farm had come to a halt. Cows in the barn stood perplexed and neglected in their wooden stanchions, turning their heads forlornly from one side to the other. Restricted movement was compensated for by their large eyes rolling slowly and hopefully in the direction of the barn door. Steam from their moist noses, or occasional droppings of dung, were in sharp contrast to the bleak cold of the night.

It was nearly evening and the wake for Tim was in noisy progress, with the small house filled to capacity. Neighbors of the Irish settlement had responded to the untimely passing of Tim (he was only 38), and the pantry shelves were stacked with food brought in by the many sympathizers. Mrs. O'Brien wouldn't have to cook for at least a week, it seemed. There were large baked hams, scalloped potatoes by the pansful, salads, several loaves of fresh bread, cakes, and some mince, apple and pumpkin pies. But more important to the affair, there was an ample supply of Irish whiskey and apple jack.

Tim was laid out in a mahogany casket in the

parlor. People came and went, paying their respects, while some stayed longer.

"It's going to be a clear, cold one tonight. Probably go down to twenty below," commented John Donovan as he prepared to leave. A gust of cold air stabbed into the kitchen when he opened the door and hastily closed it after him.

The food was good, the whiskey better, and the menfolk clustered in a group while the ladies were busy trying to comfort Mrs. O'Brien and doing the catering.

About eight o'clock one of the men said, "Let's go for a sleigh ride. It's a fine, bright night." Somehow it seemed like a wonderful idea to several of the men. They had been inside the warm house most of the afternoon and evening, and felt the need of a little exercise.

"It'll clear our heads out," said Tommy Walsh. And so they were soon dressed with their warmer clothing and ready to go outside. The O'Briens had a large hand sleigh which ordinarily would hold three comfortably, but feeling as they did it easily held five. And then there was the toboggan which could hold four or five more. Soon they were making their way up the hill toward the top. It was indeed a good night. The glazed crust on the snow glistened in the moonlight; trees, a few lofty clouds, and the barn cast shadows on its mirror-like surface. They crunched, first one foot, then the other down through the brittle topping. It was up to their waist in some places, but they didn't mind. If anyone fell, it was all in fun and no one seemed to care much how covered with snow he got. They had a wonderful time and on the third trip down, turned over in the snow at the end of the ride, laughing and calling to one another. Then someone said, "There's only one thing wrong with this."

"What's that?" said Ed Harney. "Tim O'Brien should be here enjoying this with us, instead of tucked off in that velvet-lined casket," said Dan Murphy. "You're absolutely right," said Frank Burke. "He should be out here with us." Then, all agreed, they plodded over toward the house. Warmth gushed out when they opened the door. The ladies washing dishes laughed when they saw them come in. "Land o'livin', look at them, like snowmen!"

One of the men laughed, his face ruddy with cold. He took off his horsehide mittens and clapped his hands together, then blew warmth on them. "Get Tim's overcoat, we're taking him out with us," he declared. "What!" exclaimed one of the ladies. "You're all raving mad, Frank Burke." The other men gave support to what Frank said. "Why not?" they asked. "It's fittin' he should be riding down the slope with us, his old friends. What better way to see him through?"

Despite the protests from some of the women, Tim was carefully lifted out of the casket and propped against a chair while they dressed him in his overcoat, boots, hat, scarf, and mittens. "There, old Tim, now you're ready," said Frank. The men carried him outdoors and over to the sled. "You hold him on the sled, boys," said Tommy, "while Ben O'Shea and I pull."

They moved slowly up the hill, enjoying themselves more than ever. Each man was warm and comfortable again, refortified from a drink or two while they were in the house.

"Look up on that hill," exclaimed one of the ladies, who had pulled back the curtain from a kitchen window. "They're coming down now." The men's voices sounded loud and clear in the frosty night as they sped down the hill, holding Tim O'Brien. They came to a slow halt at the bottom near the milkhouse.

The sledding party continued until after midnight. Finally, with scolding and pleading from the women, they came back to the house, carrying Tim with them. The ladies had to admit it hadn't done Tim any harm. He looked more peaceful, more satisfied resting there in the coffin after having been out for one last fling with the boys.

Nickname

Ebenezer Munson was well put together. His tall, youthful body had been made strong by hard work, and his blue eyes had a direct, uncluttered look. Bill Vail had hired and fired enough men to know that here was a good man. Ebenezer introduced himself a little self-consciously.

"Where do you hail from?" asked Mr. Vail.

"Vermont, sir."

"What kind of work are you looking for?"

"I'm a blacksmith by trade," said Ebenezer.

"We already have a blacksmith here, but what else can you do?" asked Mr. Vail. He didn't want to lose this young man to some other employer.

"I worked in a sawmill in Vermont," said Ebenezer.

"If you will take a job in the sawmill, you're hired. When could you start work?"

Without hesitating, Ebenezer said, "Right now."

It was already 1835 and Ebenezer thought that if he was ever going to get ahead, this prosperous hamlet of Vail Mills in upstate New York would be a good place to settle. There were a grist mill, sawmill, box factory, blacksmith shop, and a general store. And the place was growing.

It didn't take Ebenezer long to work into the new routine, and he was liked by the other workmen at the mill. He was now busy every day except Sunday, hauling giant logs into the mill where the sharp teeth of the up-and-down saws and circular saws could be heard ringing from morning until night as they tore through the logs. In the mill yard were the constantly mushrooming mountains of golden sawdust—a by-product of a growing America.

One afternoon, two laborers were out in the yard piling up some white pine planks, occasionally talking back and forth to one another as they worked.

"Munson says he can tell any kind of wood that has ever grown in these parts by just smelling of it," said a man named Hank.

"He knows timber all right. You can see that— the way he handles the lumber here at the mill," the older man remarked as they continued their work.

Suddenly Hank said, "We ought to try and fool him. Put a blindfold on him and see if he can really tell wood by just smelling of it."

"Yeah," replied another worker who had stopped by to listen and join in the discussion. "We could get different samples like apple, hickory, and a couple of others to fool him."

They decided to gather some pieces of wood before work next day and try their trick on young Ebenezer Munson.

"Hear about what we're going to try with the new man, Munson, tomorrow?" asked one of the men who was an instigator of the plot. And then they went on to explain the plan to some of the others. "We're going to leave some pieces of wood at the store tomorrow morning, and during our break at noon we'll ask Munson to come over and prove his claim about being able to tell any piece of wood by its smell."

"He might be able to do it, too," said a good friend of Ebenezer when he heard what was up.

On the following day the general store, which was just a stone's throw from the sawmill, was the setting for real drama. Word had spread among those working in the grist mill and box factory about what was going to take place, and before noon the store was packed with spectators.

Ebenezer was quite sure of his abilities and actually looked forward to displaying his prowess. After all, couldn't he tell the difference in the smell of apple wood from spruce, or cherry from apple? Of course he could.

The noonday whistle blew loud and shrill. "Come on, Munson!" the men shouted as they started for the store. "We're going to blindfold you for this."

"All right, boys," said Ebenezer with a grin, as he walked along with some of the men. "I'd keep my eyes shut anyway, but go ahead and blindfold me."

The heavy red flannel which they used was impossible to see through and wide enough to cover Ebenezer's eyes. Chances to peek were quite impossible. They tied the cloth securely around his head, putting in an extra knot to make sure it would stay in place.

"Hey, that's tight enough!" exclaimed Ebenezer.

The men laughed and the crowd became more excited.

Hank reached down into the box which was on the floor next to the pot-bellied stove. He selected the first piece of wood. Now the entire room was hushed. You could hear the occasional crackling of the fire in the stove, and outside the voices of people seemed quite remote as they passed by, unaware of what was going on inside the general store.

Hank lifted the first stick of wood from the box and held it under Ebenezer's nose.

"Maple," said Ebenezer, seeming barely to smell of the wood.

"Yippee, he guessed the first one!" a man shouted.

The next samples were of balsam and hickory. He named them without any trouble.

"I think he's got you stumped, Hank," called one of the men.

"Here's one he won't guess," said Hank as he reached down and carefully pulled out a small cherry board.

"That's easy," said Ebenezer. "It's cherry."

By this time it began to seem as though Ebenezer would live up to his claim. The men were quite impressed, and Hank took off his cap and scratched his head. Then looking down at the almost-emptied box on the floor, he saw something which gave him an idea. A big tom cat. He watched it, almost transfixed, as the thought took shape in his mind.

In the meantime the cat, with arched back and tail up straight in the air, was rubbing hard, back and forth against his leg. Slowly Hank stooped down putting his hand under the cat's belly, lifting it up to within smelling distance of Ebenezer's nose. Ebenezer sniffed casually, then he became more intently interested. He leaned his head closer, and Hank pulled the old tom away just in time. But even now, Ebenezer's nose was only a few inches from the cat. He sniffed several times, his nose drawn up at the corners in a concentrated effort of smelling. Then very deliberately he announced, "That's beech."

The crowded room filled with laughter as one of the men hastily removed the blindfold. Hank was still holding up the cat for Ebenezer to see.

"Hi, Beech!" called one of the men. The name was picked up by the others and soon the store was ringing with calls of "Hello, Beech. Say, that's the first time I ever saw beech with fur on it. Beech is easier to say than Ebenezer!"

Ebenezer was good-natured and took the ribbing in his stride. But the nickname stuck. Long after he had settled down just a few miles from Vail Mills in a place which became known as Munsonville, he was referred to by people from far and near as Beech Munson.

See Appendix: Nickname.

Keep Turning

This story was told to a friend of mine by her grandmother, Mrs. Louisa Warner, who lived in the Village of Mayfield.

Mrs. Warner came to the United States from Canada in 1886 at the age of thirteen. She was sent to live with an aunt and uncle who at that time lived on what is now called the Mountain Road, near Northville, New York.

"During the evening there was always time for story telling as of course there was no television or radio at that time—and one of the favorite tales uncle Jim Painter told his niece was of the days when he was a logger in the vicinity of Glens Falls. His job was to fell as many trees as possible for delivery (by way of the river) and for this job he needed good men. So when he interviewed a man for the job of cutting logs he would take him over to a grindstone and ask him to turn it while he sharpened the blade of an axe. As the prospective job holder was turning the wheel Mr. Painter would take up the axe and examine the blade. If the man stopped turning the wheel he was judged by Mr. Painter to be a poor risk and sent on his way to look for employment elsewhere."

Peggy Tight Hole

One day Bert Filmer came into my real estate office to talk about listing his bungalow on Spruce Street for sale. But first he had a story to tell.

"I'll bet you never heard the story of 'Peggy Tight Hole?'" He stood beside the office counter on which I kept a receipt book, clock, an undemanding cactus in a pot of perpetually arid soil, and a spool of scotch tape. Bert, a retired leather worker, was a quiet man. He was smiling now with a sparkle in his blue eyes, as he looked at me.

I was flabbergasted for a moment. "No," I responded. "Who on earth is that?"

Bert continued, "About 1885 I was attending High School here in Gloversville. We all knew a man who became known as 'Peggy'. He did small jobs for people in the city and also sawed four-foot hardwood into one-foot lengths for stoves. He and his wife, whose name really was Peggy, lived in a small, wood frame house on Cottage Street, near the downtown area. Without his wife's money coming in, it would have been difficult for them to get along. She was a glove worker. It wasn't that he couldn't earn enough, but he had one insatiable weakness: the tavern on week-ends. It was a constant vigil for his wife to latch on to his pay before the bartender.

"On one particular Saturday night he managed to sneak out of the house and made a beeline for his favorite tavern. He had money which he had found cached away by his wife between the pages of 'My Favorite Recipes.' It was most of his week's pay.

"By ten o'clock he was drunk. He did, however, when the bartender turned him in the right direction, manage to find his way home. No lights were on in the house. He staggered along the board walk which led to the back door and turned the knob. The door was locked. Grumbling, he carefully turned the doorknob again and pulled. It was locked all right. He stumbled down the steps, listing from one side to the other as he went around to the front door. This was locked, too.

"Slowly, through his pickled stupor, came the realization of the predicament he was in. He had no keys, and the doors were locked. What would his wife say! He tried to blot that thought from his mind. Then he remembered the windows and almost fell down the porch steps in his haste to walk around the house trying first one, then the next. But these were locked too. 'She saw to that,' he muttered, cursing low and profoundly.

"Suddenly, as with most great ideas, this one seemed to come from out of nowhere—the cellar windows! There were two of them, both small. One opened into the root cellar and the other the coal bin. He would try the root cellar first. He knocked on the bottom of the wooden frame with his fist, but nothing happened. Afraid more pounding might awaken his wife, he got to his feet and went over to the other cellar window.

"Maybe she had already heard him prowling about. The thought almost froze him where he stood. But now, standing beside the bin window, he went down upon his knees, reached over and gave a push against the window frame. It swung open. Two, small, rusty hinges squeaked in the night. He winced at the sound, whispering to himself, 'Quiet!'

"The cellar window was small for a man his size. He would have to go in backwards. Slowly, he turned around and stuck first one foot through the opening and then the other. The bin was half full of coal. He began to wiggle his way in, stomach pressed flat to the ground. It was a tight fit and his feet still didn't quite touch the coal in the bin. Then the very worst thing happened: he was stuck. Caught now, up to his waist, he would have to pull himself back out. But he couldn't budge. Breathing harder, he propped himself up on his elbows for leverage and pushed forward with all his strength. But he was firmly lodged in the small opening.

"Sweat bubbled from his forehead. All kinds of fears now rushed through his mind. Would the tightness begin to shut off his circulation? What if his wife found him here? What would the neighbors say?

"When his legs and feet began to prickle as he hung there, half in, half out, he gave up. First in a whimper, then in a frenzied bellow he called, 'Peggy, Peggy, help! I'm in a tight hole.' He repeated to call several times.

"His wife and then the neighbors were aroused. Soon a cluster of people gathered about him, lighted by a flickering kerosene lantern someone was carrying.

"It took several minutes, but finally they eased him free of the window opening; his wife standing by all the time, scolding.

"The story was all over town next day. For us at school he became, and always remained, Peggy Tight Hole."

See Appendix: Peggy Tight Hole.

A Church From Devil's Money

The mellowed red brick church with white wood trim always appeared an appropriate part of the scenery. Set back from the road among ancient maples and remarkably well preserved, the church has a large doorway with a fan-shaped window spreading gracefully above it. On either side of this center section is the basic rectangular body of the building. There, evenly spaced and inserted, are brick arches around high, narrow windows. All of it has a dignified effect although diminished somewhat by the fact that a tornado once blew off the steeple.

When the church was built in the last decades of the 19th century, there was no question about buying an organ for it. That would have been much too frivolous for the thrifty farmers of the section— descendants of Scotsmen who had settled the region in the 1760's. Residents of this area around Perth, in Fulton County, lived in simple elegance in their stout, comfortable houses, still in good condition after generations of use. It was a setting that seemed matter-of-fact and typical with nothing unusual or romantic about it.

Natives, however, often tell of the intriguing background of the solid brick church as they relate the extraordinary experience of two maiden ladies of the neighborhood.

Miss Hannah, three years older than her sister, Alice, had straight black hair which she parted in the middle and pulled severely back, fastening it in a large bun at the nape of her neck. Miss Alice's blonde hairline started well back on an extremely high forehead. Everyone knew she curled her hair but she tried to keep it a secret. In the privacy of her room she heated slim slate pencils over an oil lamp until they were hot, then curled her hair around them, one slate at a time. The resulting ringlike tubes were arranged, six on each side, coming just below her ears. Also, trying to lower her hairline, she placed a long curl the width of her forehead.

By the time the sisters reached middle age, both their mother and father had died, leaving them suddenly in possession of a large farm, free and clear from debt, and a considerable amount of cash. The girls had been raised in a puritanical atmosphere but this move into control of the family fortune had an unsettling effect upon them. So long sheltered and content to go no further than the county in which they were born, they now decided to take a trip—not just to Schenectady or Albany, but to Europe!

It was astounding to observe the slow but gradual change taking place in them as they made preparations to sail. Most of their clothes were home made, but they decided to splurge and buy two new dresses in Schenectady. One characteristic of each garment was its severity. They both preferred high-collared dresses and blouses, so there were no daring necklines to be found in the large steamer trunks when they were packed.

When actually underway, the farther they slipped from their native surroundings the more they shed the heavy weight of pious respectability. Even if many of the people they met on board ship did seem "loose," they were pleasant, and by the time the vessel docked at Le Havre the two maiden ladies were feeling quite worldly and anticipated with great excitement the trip on the continent.

They never could become fully accustomed to the

habits of the French, but learned a few words of the language. By the time they reached the Riviera these two eccentric American ladies were receiving much attention from the attentive French.

Miss Hannah and Miss Alice had heard of Monte Carlo. If anyone told them a few weeks ago they would contemplate gambling in the Casino they would have been shocked. But now, making their way to a roulette table in the luxurious, mirrored casino, it seemed as though it had always been permissible.

However, still not so intoxicated with Gallic warmth as to forget their conservative background, the two sisters registered their name and address, buying just five dollars worth of chips between them. They enjoyed the game, but it did seem too easy, and, as the evening progressed, they caused quite a stir among the more sophisticated at the Casino.

Toward midnight they decided it was time to return to the hotel. They got up, said good-bye to the croupier and prepared to leave the casino.

"But, mesdames, your winnings!" exclaimed the croupier.

At the mention of money the ladies bristled. "We didn't play for money—just to see what the casino was like and to pass the time." Then they turned and walked sedately and surely out of the casino in the wake of the amazed stares of the croupier and the little crowd of people who had gathered around the table.

By now the manager had come over to the table and, after learning what happened, went to call the ladies back. But they had disappeared into the warm starlit night.

The following morning the casino manager himself proceeded to check the local hotels, in search of the two women. It was the law: all winnings had to be paid.

Hannah and her sister Alice had not lived on a farm all their lives without forming some irrevocable habits. When the casino manager finally located the hotel where they stayed, the desk clerk informed him the two mesdames had checked out very early that morning. "Very early indeed," repeated the clerk, shrugging his shoulders and giving the manager a 'these impossible-Americans' look.

The sisters continued to enjoy a full itinerary on the continent and after three months sailed for the United States. They arrived home in August and settled back into the regular routine almost as if nothing had happened. Certainly the neighbors couldn't notice any change in the sisters. However, there were times, at home, or at a quilting bee or some other function, when they exchanged secretive glances which spoke of other times and places.

One day, toward the end of September, a knock was heard at the door of their large, brick house. Martha, the housekeeper, answered.

"What did you say your name was?" she was heard to ask with a note of disbelief in her voice.

"Monsieur Bossard," came the reply.

Poor Martha, a large, spare woman, tried unsuccessfully to repeat the name, then said belligerently, "You sellin' somethin'?

"No! No! No! Now tell me please, is this the home of the Mesdames —?" the foreigner asked, mentioning the family name.

"Yes, it is," said Martha grudgingly.

"Then, please, may I speak to the ladies? I have come a long way to see them."

"Well, come in," said Martha, still skeptical and hardly opening the door wide enough for Monsieur Bossard to enter.

"You wait here, I'll get 'em," she said, and went off toward the rear of the large house, leaving Monsieur Bossard standing in the hall.

When Martha found Miss Alice and Miss Hannah

46

in the sewing room, she told them about the caller, sounding as if he were someone from another planet. "I think," she said in Miss Hannah's ear, "He's a Frenchman!"

"A Frenchman!" repeated Miss Hannah, looking at her sister, who returned her anxious glance over some crochet work.

The sisters stood up, hurriedly patted their hair and looked down at their dresses, straightening a bow here or a pleat there and then walked toward the door leading to the entrance hall. The three of them advanced toward the stranger.

"Mesdames —?" inquired the Frenchman politely, yet with a note of anxiety in his voice.

Miss Hannah, who usually acted as spokesman, said "Yes. What is it you want young man?"

"I'm Monsieur Bossard from Monte —"

He was interrupted by Miss Hannah, whose voice was now tinged with terror. Someone from Monte Carlo! She thought, I must send Martha out of here, she'll spread this all over the place.

"Just a moment," she said to the stranger. Turning to Martha she asked, "Martha, will you fix tea for us? I'll ring when we are ready."

"Yes, Miss Hannah," said Martha, then went off

somewhat reluctantly. She was beginning to get interested in all this.

"Will you please come in and sit down?" asked Hannah, leading the way toward the large parlor.

"Thank you," said Monsieur Bossard, as he walked into the room, continuing his introduction. "I was sent here by the management of the Casino at Monte Carlo."

The word Monte Carlo again stabbed at the ladies and a ghost from the past, much better left there, was suddenly brought to life.

Alice surprised herself by asking rather weakly, "What could you possibly want with us?"

"I came all this way to give you your winnings. It is the rule of the Casino and money must be given to the rightful owners. We can't keep it."

Hannah decided it was time for a serious talk with this man. "Mr. Bossard, you must understand this: we came into your Casino merely to see what it was like. We don't believe in gambling and couldn't take any winnings that night, nor can we take them now."

"But ladies," protested Monsieur Bossard, little beads of perspiration showing on his forehead while he listened, almost unbelieving, to Miss Hannah.

"Do you know the amount?"

"No," said Miss Hannah, and Miss Alice shook her head to signify her ignorance of the whole affair.

"It is $7,600. and I must leave this draft on a New York City bank with you."

The sisters looked at one another without saying a word. This was indeed a lot of money. How could they have ever won such an amount by just sitting at a table in the Casino, placing five dollars worth of chips on different numbers?

Suddenly Hannah had an idea. "Excuse us, Mr. Bossard. My sister and I would like to talk for a moment, please." Then she said to Alice, "Will you come into the east livingroom with me a minute?"

When they were out of Monsieur Bossard's hearing, Alice blurted out, "It's Devil's money. We can't take it. If anyone should ever find out!"

"The young man seems quite in earnest, Alice. And I have an idea," said Miss Hannah.

"What do you mean?" exclaimed Miss Alice.

"We need a church here at Perth. Why couldn't we donate the money for a new church?"

It sounded like the answer to a prayer to Miss Alice. "Oh, yes! yes!" she cried. "Then we can accept it and get rid of the Frenchman."

The two ladies walked back into the parlor,

victorious. "We have decided to accept the money, Mr. Bossard. But first let us assure you, we would never keep it for ourselves." And Miss Hannah told him of their plan.

This was indeed incredulous to their visitor, but he was glad to make delivery and would ask no questions.

After tea and a polite but brief conversation, Monsieur Bossard was on his way.

Just before he left, Miss Hannah said, almost in a whisper so her sister and Martha couldn't hear, "We did enjoy ourselves in your country, Monsieur!"

See Appendix: A Church From Devil's Money.

A Fish House Story

Sunday afternoon in April, 1976, my wife and I visited the home of Mr. and Mrs. Louis Sleezer at the Fish House. We knew of Mrs. Sleezer's interest in the history of the area and had wanted to meet her. She is extremely knowledgeable about that area of upstate New York, but it was from her husband that I heard an unusual story.

Before continuing it will be good to note that Mr. Sleezer said he is a decendant of Godfrey Shew, who in 1762 was the first permanent white settler of the Fish House. The afternoon sped by talking with someone whose family had lived in one area for over 200 years. It gave a validity to anything Mr. Sleezer told us about the history of the place, including the following anecdote.

Time: turn of the century on a winter's morning.

Place: Fish House in the Sacandaga Valley, New York.

Characters: Mr. Osborn, Mr. Brown and a snowplow man.

Other characters: a horse.

In those days the Fish House boasted of at least two hotels, the Osborn Hotel and the Fish House Hotel. Mr. Brown was proprietor of the latter hotel and Mr. Osborn proprietor of the hotel which bore his name.

It had finally stopped snowing the morning of the incident and the flakes, cold and crystaline, caught the sunlight, covering the ground with a jewel-like blanket. Outstretched boughs of evergreen trees were layered in tiers of billowy white; occasionally a piece would break off, sifting downward through the branches to dapple the snow beneath. Pillars of smoke rose straight up from chimneys in the village.

One of the first roadways to be plowed was that on the village square which had a hotel located on either side. The man whose job it was to keep the road open was already at work, coaxing his horse on as the plow cleaved through the snow.

Mr. Osborn came out on the hotel porch and was disturbed with what he saw. The snow was

54

being plowed onto the walkway which had been cleared from in front of his hotel earlier that morning. With his breath steaming from the cold as he talked he called, "Don't plow the snow back on the walkway here. It has just been shoveled!"

The plowman waved his arm in recognition of this request. Upon reaching the Fish House Hotel, Mr. Brown, who had come out on the porch, asked the plowman why he hadn't cleared all of the road. The man told him that Mr. Osborn had forbid him to do so.

Mr. Brown, after hearing what the man said called, "Wait a minute, I'll be right out," and he went inside. He was soon back on the porch with his rifle.

"Come on," he said as he jumped onto the plow. "We will go over there and clear the road." With some reluctance, which he kept to himself, the plowman started toward the other side of the square.

Mr. Osborn was ready and waiting. He was unmindful of the cold as he stood there on the porch in his shirt sleeves. "Don't either of you come any further with that plow!" he commanded as the two men neared the hotel.

"Pay him no heed," urged Mr. Brown as they continued on their way.

The snowplow man had regained some confidence and, nearing the unplowed area, slapped his horse with the reins as he called, "gee! gee!"

Mr. Osborn grabbed a snow shovel leaning against the porch railing and ran down the steps. Racing toward the horse, he brought it down with a forceful "whack" upon the animal's head.

Mr. Brown, now infuriated with what was happening, raised his rifle, aimed it at Mr. Osborn and pulled the trigger. The range was close and the bullet found its mark, killing Mr. Osborn in his tracks.

Indian at the Window

My grandmother, Elizabeth Dennie Abbey, was born at Dennie Hollow, Mayfield. She weighed three pounds at birth and they carried her around on a pillow. This small beginning had nothing to do with durability, she lived to be ninety-four years old. Among other things, I remember her for her sugar cookies and her stories. She related the following incident which I've never forgotten:

It was a sunny July day near Mayfield, New York, a small settlement at the Adirondack foothills. Johnny heard his mother cry, "Indians! Hurry, Johnny hurry!"

Heart pounding, Johnny Wilkins stood motionless for a second, then dropping his fishing pole he turned from the creek bank and ran toward the cabin. Run for the cornfield, he thought. The stalks had begun to tassle and were high enough to hide most of him.

He felt a little safer, once he was among the cornstalks. Only his yellow hair could occasionally be seen bobbing above the green spears as he ran. Crouching to keep his head low the long blades lashed, rough as a cat's tongue, against his face as he hurried on.

Mrs. Wilkins, standing a short distance from the cabin, cried out again. She knew Johnny had gone fishing but as her eyes scanned the field and down toward the creek, she wondered if he had gone farther downstream. His father had told him not to go too far away from the house until he was back from Johnstown. Why, she mused, did it have to be today he went into the village? It was only early afternoon and would probably be sundown before he returned.

Mrs. Wilkins looked across the meadow at the Indian as he made his way out of the forest and toward the cabin. He looked larger than ever now, as he came closer. His red body glistened with sweat and he carried a tomahawk. At that instant, hearing the rustle of corn stalks, she turned her eyes from the Indian, toward the cornfield. Were there more Indians coming from another direction?

It was Johnny. She saw his bright blond hair and tanned face pushing toward her through the

60

corn, his brown eyes wide with excitement. Breaking his way out of the cornfield he rushed up to her. There was no time for greetings, and casting a backward glance at the Indian, they raced toward the cabin.

"Slam!" went the door, as Mrs. Wilkins closed it after them. Down went the wooden cross-bar, locking the door securely into place.

Johnny had been running so fast he could scarcely find the breath to ask, "Is there just one Indian? How many more?"

"That's all I saw, Johnny," said his mother, holding him close to her for a moment, as she leaned with her back against the door. "But hurry, we must make sure the wooden shutters on the windows are barred. I'm glad we closed them before your father left this morning, just in case something did happen."

They hurriedly examined the shutters, trying each one to make sure they were barred. "This one in the store room doesn't have any shutters on it," called Johnny in alarm.

It was true, it didn't have any shutters on, and the window was hanging open on its leather hinges to let air into the room. Mr. Wilkins had added the small area after the cabin had been built Johnny remembered, because he had watched and even helped his father build it. There was a narrow doorway just to the right of the fireplace which opened into the little room. They used it as a place to store things such as maple sugar, flour, potatoes, beef jerky, herbs, salt pork and other foods. And Mrs. Wilkins kept her butter churn there. The little window at the end of the room was too high from the ground for most anyone to reach. Anyone would have to be awfully thin to get through that window, thought Johnny. That was why they had never made shutters for it.

Johnny and his mother went over and peeked through a crack between the boards of the door. "Can you see the Indian?" asked Johnny, pressing his face harder against the sliver of light. He couldn't see much from where he stood, but his mother might be able to see more. Maybe higher the crack was wider.

"No, I can't see him," she said uneasily, as she peered outside. You don't know where the savage is or what he is up to, she thought. And then, too, had any other Indians joined him after she and Johnny entered the cabin?

Listening carefully, Johnny whispered, "I hear footsteps by the front of the cabin."

His mother could barely hear the soft moccasin step of the Indian, then, "Bang!" as he brought his fist down mightily upon the door.

"Ma, where's the gun?"

Gathering Johnny closer to her she said, "We haven't a gun in the cabin. Your Pa took it into the village gunsmith today for repair."

Suddenly the loud banging upon the door stopped. All was quiet. Just the chirping of crickets from underneath the big rock in front of the cabin.

"Where has he gone now?" asked Johnny. Then, as if in answer to his question they heard a thudding noise against the side of the cabin. It had come from the storeroom.

"Maybe he really can get in there," cried Johnny, at the same time looking around the cabin to see if there wasn't something they could use with which to defend themselves. Then he saw something. "Ma" he said, "the axe. We can use Pa's axe!"

But Mrs. Wilkins was so busy with her own thoughts she didn't hear Johnny.

The next instant they saw four strong red fingers curve over and grip the inside of the window sill. Then the tips of two Indian headdress feathers appeared in the storeroom window.

"We will have to use it Ma, we've just got to," said Johnny.

"Use what?" said Mrs. Wilkins, trying to control her voice and not show how frightened she was.

"The axe, the big one Pa uses to cut trees with."

There was no time to lose. Johnny ran over to the axe which was leaning against the wall, right next to the doorway. It was heavy as he lifted it from the floor, big metal head bumping against his shins while he used both hands to carry it over to his mother.

Mrs. Wilkins took courage from her son's action, and grabbing the axe from his hands, ran into the storeroom. She lifted the big axe with all her strength and brought it down across the fingers whch were curled over the edge of the window sill. There was a painful cry as they heard the Indian fall to the ground. Then, as his moans became more distant, they knew he had gone.

Mrs. Wilkins felt so weak, she just couldn't stand up any longer. She slumped down upon the edge of the butter churn.

"His fingers," said Johnny, "Two of his fingers were cut off!"

After a while Johnny and his mother decided it was safe to open the large door, and they stepped out into the sunlight. It had been dark inside the cabin with the shutters closed, and they blinked from the brightness.

Later, when they saw Mr. Wilkins trudging across the field toward home with a bag of flour across his shoulders and the rifle in his hand, they rushed to meet him. "Pa, an Indian tried to get us this afternoon!" shouted Johnny, before reaching his father.

Mr. Wilkins lowered the heavy bag of flour to the ground. He placed his gun against it just in time to catch Johnny who made a running jump into his arms. Mr. and Mrs. Wilkins looked anxiously at one another for a moment, then Mr. Wilkins held Johnny a little closer. He said softly, "Talk a little slower, son. I can scarcely understand what you're saying."

After a minute or two, Mr. Wilkins lowered Johnny to the ground and picked up the gun and bag of flour. They walked toward the cabin together while Johnny told his father everything that had happened.

See Appendix: Indian At The Window.

The Amah's Prayer

Shanghai still seems far removed from Gloversville, in upstate New York where I live and had a real estate business. Even in the age of jets and missiles, it has an aura of excitement and mystery. I never expected some of this ancient city's color would be brought to me by my former next door neighbor, Jacob Gurowitz, proprietor of Jack's Ready to Wear Shop.

For us, activity slows down during the winter months, allowing time for reading, visiting and some reflection. The elements seem to conspire toward this end, with banks of snow and below-zero weather making us draw within ourselves to find a microcosm of warmth. It was during this long winter lull that, seated one morning near a sizzling radiator at the rear of Jack's store, I heard of an incident which happened while he was living in China.

"I was born in Shanghai but my parents took

me to Russia, their homeland, when I was a youngster. A few years later, with the Russian Revolution imminent, I returned to China alone. It was possible for me to leave because I wasn't a native-born Russian. After arriving in Shanghai I obtained work as a clerk with an import-export firm.

"The pension where I lived was located in the thickly populated International Settlement, not far from the Whampoo River. French, English, Russian, Italian—most any nationality you might mention, lived in this section of the city. The structure was wedged into a row of similar two and three story buildings with stucco and wood facades, strung along a narrow, cobblestone street. The pension contained quarters for the owner and his family, a large dining room, kitchen and fourteen rooms for rent. Employed at the pension was a male cook, a coolie and an amah.

"What's an amah?" I asked.

"An old Chinese woman who does work around the house. A little floor cleaning, a little washing, in fact everything she does a little. She's usually too old for much vigorous work. In the pension she did a little sweeping, some laundry, and slept on the first floor, under the stairs.

"Our amah was a small, spare woman with a

face like a wrinkled apple. Her feet were bound in the old Chinese custom and she shuffled around in an unassuming way, yet maintained a lively inconspicuous interest in the activities of the lodgers at the pension.

"One day a man and woman, claiming to be actors, came to rent a room. They had been with a theatrical company up in the northern part of China. The tour was over and they were now back to enjoy the more sophisticated atmosphere of the city. Their room was next to mine, and through the thin walls in the house I could hear everything they said. Their voices were especially loud and audible and the crescendo of gaiety or violent arguing was quite revealing for one used to a less bohemian life. At first I found it all very interesting, but after a couple of days wished the room had been occupied by a less emotional couple who would keep reasonable hours.

"Of all the people in the pension, the amah was most disturbed by this pair and when they passed her in the hall or on the stairs, she wouldn't recognize their presence. Even if they spoke to her, she kept her eyes downcast to avoid theirs. Her only sign of recognition was a faint, fleeting grimace.

"Everyone was relieved the day they left. Late

that same afternoon I came home from work and as I approached the room occupied by them, I was startled to see smoke seeping out from beneath the door and into the hallway. Rushing over, I threw open the door, expecting to see the place in flames. Instead, there was the old amah kneeling on the floor, praying at an improvised altar of burning incense. Each room had its wash basin and she was using this as a receptacle for the smouldering pyre. 'What are you doing, praying in here?' I yelled.

"'I'm praying they will die,' she said.

"But why should you pray they will die? What have they done to you?' I asked her.

"'They have gone and left me nothing. Not even five cents.' she declared bitterly.

"You see," my friend explained, "It was the custom to tip the amah when checking out of a pension.

"'Would you kill someone for just five cents?' I asked, finding her eyes with mine and holding them. 'Here, here is ten cents for you.' And I handed her the money.

"'No, no, I wouldn't kill anyone for five cents,' she cried, as though the thought of actually committing such a deed appalled her.

"'But that's what you're praying—that they will die.'

"She knelt there on the floor for a few seconds with head bowed and said nothing more. Then she looked up at me, her brown eyes brimming with tears, 'Oh, no, master, I didn't mean to kill anyone.' Then she hastily put the smudge out with her bare hands, got up and left the room, taking the basin of burned incense with her.

"As the days went by I noticed the amah looked more distracted, almost ill. I feared for her health. Then one day when I came home from my office, she met me at the door. It seemed impossible such an old, careworn face could become so radiant.

"'They are alive! Master Jack they're alive!' she cried, and then a few large teardrops began an irregular course down her ancient cheeks.

"She explained that that very morning she had visited a friend, an amah at another pension in Shanghai, and while there her friend spoke of a man and woman, claiming to be actors, who were living at the pension. After listening to her friend's complaints about the pair, she became excited. Learning they never got up until late and would be coming out of their room about noontime, the old amah waited anxiously to catch a glimpse of them.

71

Eventually they came down the stairs, passing her on their way outside.

"'I saw them!' she exclaimed. 'I didn't kill them for five cents,' she told me jubilantly.

"I assured her it was indeed good tidings to learn the actors were alive.

"'Yes, it's good I didn't pray hard enough for them to die. It's good,' she said simply, as she turned and walked away.

See Appendix: The Amah's Prayer.

Tied to Mother's Apron Strings

Before reaching my teen years, I remember our family would consider it one of the high points of the week to plan a trip with the automobile. In those days, mid twenties, it was exciting to contemplate packing a picnic lunch on Sunday and climbing into that still magical conveyance, the auto, to journey northward for the day. The adirondack area was our destination. Usually it would be in the direction of Northville, Wells and Lake Pleasant. We always found a place along the road to spread a tablecloth—more often than not underneath the pines alongside the Sacandaga River. We all took part in selecting the spot. Mother would call to my father who was driving the car, "There's a nice shaded place up ahead in that clearing." Usually we had a friend or relative with us, who helped in selecting a suitable site. I recall those brilliant summer days, not a cloud to mar the blue sky. It was dazzling. The air had a newness, with the sun drawing an essence from the pines that engulfed us from all sides with its needled aroma.

To reach these places in the Adirondack foothills my father usually took the road from Gloversville, where we lived, to Northville and then northward. This meant we would pass the home of widow Blane and hear a story which remains with me to this day, as it does with many other natives and older residents of the region.

What made this small, two story wood frame house near the side of the road special was its inhabitants. Everyone knew the widow had been left alone to raise her sons. At first the household seemed normal enough with its day to day chores, school for the two small boys and church on Sunday. Then the people in the vicinity noticed a change. The older son no longer attended school. He didn't come to Sunday School and his playmates found he wasn't available to play the usual games or go fishing, climb trees, or swim in the nearby Sacandaga River.

Questions began to be raised, along with eyebrows. Where was the boy? Curiosity naturally got the best of some neighbors and they called on the widow and asked about the lad. She invited them into the house, but not to see the boy. It was then they learned he was in bed and had been there for several days. "Yes, he's ailin'—too sick and weak to get out of bed and maybe catch something else," was the mother's lament.

No doctor had been called to examine the boy. The mother said she could care for him. This went on for months, perhaps a year and then one day an ominous thing happened: the second son did not appear in school nor was he there in the days to follow.

Other neighbors were by this time concerned and called on the widow. They were not invited to come in but met at the door and informed her second son also had fallen victim of some disease and that he too was now confined to bed where he was to remain until well again.

Weeks, months, and then years passed and the two boys remained in bed, completely dependent upon their mother's care. They grew into young manhood never coming outdoors where they might "catch something." Rumors spread. Some said the boys were chained to their beds and couldn't leave the house.

Some have said that after the mother died they

were left to fend for themselves. It took time, but eventually they were able to take part in the affairs around them, marry and have a regular family life.

Maybe this story is all fiction, as the name of the widow. Where and with whom it originated I suppose no one knows. It has become part of the region's folk legacy and seems assured of being told and retold, with each telling changed to reflect the genre of the teller.

The Unfortunate Pig

This generation has no corner on caring for, and protecting members of the animal kingdom. Other people, long ago, cared as much as many of us do now. This was brought to my attention by the account of a woman who lived on a small farm at the foothills of the Adirondack Mountains. It wasn't far from the Gloversville city limits and was reached by a narrow dirt road.

My friend, the teller of this story, said he didn't want names mentioned. The woman was a distant relative of his and she still had a few kinsmen living in the area.

"She loved all kinds of animals," he said, beginning the story at the scene of the old, two story wood frame farmhouse. "I remember they said she even fed the rats that would come around the wood shed. She also kept pigs and other barnyard animals. Cows, a horse, chickens and like that," he continued.

"One of the sows was due any time. This was looked forward to with great anticipation by the owner. Day by day the progress of the pig was observed until, late one night, the piglets arrived. They were all squealing with healthy hunger as they competed for their mother's milk. All except one— the runt of the litter. It was so sickly the owner wondered if it would survive, so she decided to care for it in the house. The little pig was kept warm and well fed. Days of loving attention finally produced results. The puny piglet grew strong and in the meantime the lady became very attached to it. In fact so much so that the pig became a household pet.

"And you know you can't housebreak a pig," said my friend.

"This lady had a son and daughter-in-law who lived upstairs in the house. Maybe they had made a two family dwelling out of the place, I don't know. Anyway, the pig liked her son and would go upstairs to visit him. This was fine except the pig couldn't go down the stairs by itself. So each time the pig was ready to leave, the son would have to carry it back down the steps to his mother's.

"It became larger and larger, as pigs do, and the day came when it was almost more than the son could do to carry it down the stairs. He decided something had to be done.

"A family meeting was called without the mother's knowledge. They reasoned the pig would never be happy to go back into a pigpen. It was accustomed to an entirely different way of life. While other pigs wallowed about in the muck the pet pig had been kept spotless with its skin glowing pink beneath clean white bristles. After much deliberation a decision was made: the pig had to go. However they knew their mother wouldn't consent to this voluntarily.

"'The only thing I know is to get her to go down to the city and visit Aunt Mary for the day. While she's there we will take the pig to the slaughter house,'" said the son.

"These whispered arrangements were made and carried out. When she returned to the farmhouse from spending the day with Aunt Mary in the city there were no familiar grunts to greet her. The pig was gone."

See Appendix: The Unfortunate Pig.

Bill Strait, a Vignette

I recall Bill Strait, who lived in our town, with a clarity provoked by few. There were other of its citizens who had lived illustrious, exemplary lives achieving wealth, educational degrees, and had been most charitable to institutions with life-size statues erected to perpetuate their memory. But Bill was with us every day of the year.

Most of my adult life was centered in the business section of downtown where my father had a real estate office and then, later, when I went into the business, we had the office together. We saw Bill about every day on our way to work, sometimes during the day, or on the way home. He was visible—you couldn't miss him. His occupation was gathering papers in his pushcart. He collected them from business places, homes, and then sold them to a junk dealer. Occasionally he would use his cart to make deliveries for people. The old cart with its large, spoked, metal wheels could be heard clanking noisily over the pavement as he pushed it along.

Bill, I recall, didn't travel on the sidewalk with his cart but considered it just as important a vehicle as the automobile, and entitled to the roadway. He had witnessed the advent of the auto and remembered the days when the streets were relatively quiet. Now his territory was increasingly infringed upon and he was fighting a losing battle. As he grew older and traffic became more congested, he resented the horns blowing and the closeness of the cars as they passed him. His vocabulary was limited but in the area of curse words he excelled and showed no restraint as he yelled, and shook his fists at passing motorists who drove too close or playfully called out some demeaning taunt. All things considered, walking his pushcart through the city streets rain or shine, muttering to himself, cursing the motorists, and wearing unkempt clothes set him apart.

He knew my father, whose given name was James, and apparently liked him. I'm sure those occasional donations dad made to slake Bill's thirst on a hot day were one of the reasons for this preferred status my father held.

I don't know where Bill lived, or where he went

each night with his pushcart. I suspect it was near the downtown area. He was always alone. Maybe people thought it would lower their status in the community if they were found fraternizing with Bill.

One day he came into our office. I was there, and he asked me, "Is Jimmie here?" I told him he was around somewhere and at that moment my father walked into the reception room from his office.

Bill's appearance was not very tidy. It was a warm day and a cap was half cocked on his sweaty head. A horn blew outside; he stiffened as if threatened. Glancing toward the street he grumbled, "Those damn cars, they can all go to hell." He sidled over to my father and looked up at him. His large, brown eyes, one slightly askew, had a childish, trusting look. "Jimmie," he asked, "Can I have a quarter for a cold drink?"

As I have said, there were many good, upright men—outstanding in the community. How is it Bill moves right in and sits down beside these illustrious gentlemen? Maybe it's because he was unique and so much a part of the city's daily life. The more conforming, famous sons were busy plying back and forth from one country to another, occupied within the confines of their business or profession.

It will never happen, but wouldn't it be something if a statue were erected to Bill? It might read, "Here was a man who served us well and gave us a moment of superiority at the sacrifice of his own."

Once Upon a Time

The incidence seemed incredulous as my mother-in-law, Marion Dye Finch, related a few fragmented details about the Cromwell twins who had lived in New York City. Their ties with Broadalbin, New York, were through their parents and other relatives. The Husteds and Cromwells were "summer people" of the village. Not the transient kind, but people who had substantial homes in the community and were a respected, participating part of the village's life. The Husteds had a beautiful home on Maple Street. Colonel Husted was an uncle to the twins and his sister, Miss M. K. "Kitty" Husted, an aunt.

I began bombarding Marion with questions about the twins at which point she said, "Jim will be able to tell us more about them. I'll write to him in Florida where he and his aunt now live."

This she did and her letter was answered promptly. Our back yards adjoined and the day the letter arrived Marion saw me in my yard and asked if I wanted to come over when I finished working and read what Jim had to say. I can't vouch for the accuracy of the letter's contents and have eliminated some references which are personal in nature. The opinions expressed were strictly Jim's. I eagerly began to read:

"Thanks for your letter.

"Miss Husted was a dear—so good to everyone. When I was a boy in Choir School she used to send Miss Wood and the car and take me to the movies and often had me to lunch—930 Park Avenue, as I remember.

"The Titian was purchased abroad by the Chambers for an original and when Mrs. Chambers became so short of money she began to sell things—her most valuable possession being the Titian. 'Charles of London' on 57th St. in N. Y. was one of the most reputable places in N. Y. I guess and was owned by Sir Charles Duveen—his nephew was the one I knew and he was a well known authority and did the appraising for the gallery. I expect Mrs. C. asked them to appraise the painting and Albert went up to Broadalbin. He said it was very hard to have to tell her that it was not real, just a good copy and was worth nothing in comparison to what the original would have been. He said it almost broke her heart as she had been counting on the money.

"The bell on the table at 'On-a-Knoll' was supposedly the work of Benvenuto Cellini in which case it would have been almost priceless but it very well could have turned out to be a fake too. Cousin Jessie got it abroad from a museum and had the papers to go with it but who knows.

"The brick house (Beers house to us) was built by my great grandfather, Samuel Thompson and my grandmother was married from there. He was a prosperous paper manufacturer and the mill was at Stevers Mills. As a boy I remember across the creek was what remained of a very handsome old house where the family went in the summer and behind it was the remains of the slave quarters. He ran the mill with 40 slaves.

"Colonel bought the brick house from my Great Grandfather, they sent up horses and carriages, servants, etc. and entertained N. Y. friends lavishly."

Jim's mother's maiden name was Lilias Littlejohn, who at one time lived in Broadalbin. He writes: "Lilias' father and mother died and at 18 she went to England to live with her aunt, Jennie Littlejohn Husted. She spent several miserable years there, completely unaccustomed to that sort of living. She remembers they were entertained at Glamis Castle when the present Queen mother was a little girl. Finally her Aunt settled a monthly sum on her and sent her back to an aunt on the other side of the family in Elmsford, N.Y. and she married from here to my Father.

"I do not remember the names of the Cromwell twins but it was a great tragedy.

"I can tell you a lot more when I see you but I'm sure you're worn out with all this by now."

The letter was dated April 13, 1970.

Unfortunately Jim passed away before Mrs. Finch or I could obtain additional information and anecdotes about Broadalbin and some of its people from such an informed source.

By now my curiosity had been thoroughly aroused regarding the Cromwell twins and I couldn't let the subject drop. However, if I were to learn more it would be on my own. It seemed the New York Public Library would be a good place to start. After reviewing a few years of microfilm I finally found the first of several articles about the twins. The year was 1919. Also, in the newspaper morgue of a Gloversville, New York daily paper, I found an edition of a "morning newspaper," now out of print, which carried coverage I was seeking.

In my search, questions I had regarding the twins were answered, while other questions were raised and not answered. Perhaps that is the right reserved for all of us. On that final moment of reckoning our innermost thoughts belong only to us.

Gladys Louise Husted Cromwell and Dorothea Katherine Cromwell were members of one of New York City's most prestigious and wealthy families. The sisters were active in social life since their debut on December 4, 1916, and were familiar figures in horse shows and on Fifth Avenue where they were often seen driving a Four-in-Hand. They had been in the service of the American Red Cross since February, 1918, most of the time at Charlons-sur-Marne, France, where they were engaged in canteen work.

Why did it happen? the war was over with the signing of the Armistice November 11, 1918. Was it because they were exhausted from their overseas duty with the Red Cross? That was the reason given by the Metropolitan newspapers, as reported from interviews. Today the happening is as unique and vexing as it was on that fateful day in January, 1919.

The twins were young women, beautiful, rich in their own right and lived together on Park Avenue. One newspaper, in a subsequent article made a retraction and gave their age as thirty-two and not twenty-five as first reported.

One can only conjecture, never be sure, as to the reasons for the final act. As Miss M. "Kitty" Husted said to my mother-in-law, and as the girls' friend said, "They worked to the point of exhaustion during their field service in France. It was a radical change from their protected way of life at home. It was just too much." It was also reported that when the canteen closed for the day the sisters would go to the evacuation hospital, where they continued working. Apparently they were often under fire from enemy guns.

CROMWELL TWINS
END LIVES
LEAP FROM SHIP

These were the front page headlines appearing in many of the nations newspapers January 25, 1919. One of the papers included a photograph of the sisters before going overseas. They were seated, reins in hand, stylish in similar riding habits.

The front page reports continued to relate the

twins were on their way home from France, where they were in Red Cross work and suffered from long strain under fire.

The news release from Bordeaux, France, on January twenty-fourth reported the Misses Gladys and Dorothea Cromwell of New York leaped from the rail of the French liner *La Lorraine* as the ship was in the Garonne River bound for New York. The steamer was opposite the Christopher Light when the young women jumped. It went on to relate both were drowned and the bodies had not been recovered.

In a January 26, 1919 newspaper there was an article on page one in which the Bordeaux Police Chief confirmed the report that the Cromwell twins committed suicide. It said they had sailed on *La Lorraine* and that friends of the twins accompanied them to the pier. It stated that the drowning was still a mystery to members of their family. Their brother believed a mistake had been made because of conflicting dispatches and a cheerful letter he had received from his sisters less than a week ago.

As additional information was received it was learned the sisters went aboard *La Lorraine* Thursday. The ship sailed early the next morning. Seven o'clock that night the sisters were seen walking arm in arm along the promenade deck. A few minutes later an American soldier on sentry duty saw them step to the rail on the portside forward. According to the sentry, one climbed over the rail and leaped into the river. The other sister followed almost before the first struck the water.

The passengers said it was fifteen minutes before the ship could be stopped and then efforts to recover the bodies failed. It was reported that the area in the river where the twins jumped was very treacherous because of the many strong eddies. Whatever went down in that particular vicinity was almost certainly lost.

It was discovered the twins left four letters in their stateroom. One was addressed to the officer in charge of the contingent of Red Cross workers returning on the ship. Another letter was to their brother and a third to his wife. The fourth letter was to a woman friend of theirs.

Some months later, May 9, 1919, it was reported the bodies of Misses Gladys and Dorothea Cromwell who leaped to their deaths into the Garonne River from the French liner steamship *La Loraine,* had been recovered. According to the message the bodies of the two women were found on the same day.

They were buried with full military honors. Miss

Gladys Cromwell was buried at La Rochelle and Miss Dorothea Cromwell at Pauillac, France.

See Appendix: Once Upon A Time.

Introduction to Four Stories

Some time ago a large, bulging manila envelope arrived in our mail box from my first wife's (nee Charlotte Finch) aunt. Opening one end and turning it upside down, out tumbled several packets of papers yellowed and fragile with age. There was a musty odor from years of storage in attics and old trunks. Many of the sheets had been gnawed by rodents along the edges, running sentences off into jagged obscurity. I discovered a few articles she had written as part of a writing assignment which were unrelated to history or folklore and poems she had composed as a young woman graduated from Vassar College, class of 1908. There were also three anecdotes of her father's, a country doctor.

The notes of her father, Dr. Henry Clement Finch, provide the basis for three of the stories which follow.

Shoo-fly, the fourth story, was told to me orally by other members of the Finch family.

The Clairvoyant

It was in late November 1857. Samuel Finch, a farmer in the Sacandaga Valley region of upstate New York, couldn't recall a more dismal, cold, wet fall evening. The inner warmth of the log cabin in which he lived with his wife Pamelia and their two young daughters, Alice and Susan, had never felt more snug. The rain, almost sleet, pelted against the cabin in waves of relentless intensity.

Suddenly above the noise of the wind and rain they heard a brittle knock on the thick, windowless door. Then a high pitched voice that seemed to intermingle and become part of the storm called, "Hello, is anyone home? Hello!"

Pamelia turned from the fireplace where she was stirring a kettle of hot potato soup for supper and looked toward the door. "Who can that be, out in the weather this time of night?" she asked her husband.

Samuel was busy pulling burdocks from the dog. They were matted in clumps high on the inside forelegs and difficult for the animal to pick off. "Maybe one of the neighbors needs something, but I don't recognize that voice," he said, standing up and walking toward the door.

Again a knock came, more urgent, then a voice, "Anyone there?"

Samuel unbolted the door and standing in the opening was a sight they'd never seen before. The girls gasped, and huddled close to their mother. Even Samuel wasn't prepared for the witch-like figure looking up at him with dark, piercing eyes. Her greying hair protruded in curled, wet strands from under a black, hooded cape.

"Mister," said the woman, cocking her head sideways as she spoke. "I'm a stranger in these parts and don't know where to find lodging."

"Come in," said Pamelia who, with Alice and Susan, had joined Samuel by the door. "You are soaked. Come in and dry off by the fire."

"Yes, come. I'll close the door and keep the rain out," said Samuel, stepping aside.

The stranger advanced a few steps inside the cabin and looked around her. A table was set for the evening meal and the cabin, though not large, was neat and warm. A large fireplace, logs burning brightly, cast a flickering glow about the room.

She is a sight, thought Pamelia as she said to the woman, "My word, you are drenched. Come over here and stand by the fire. We will drape your cloak over a chair to dry. You should take off those shoes and stockings too," she continued, looking down at their uninvited guest's wet feet. "Alice, go into the bedroom and get that pair of slippers from the chest."

Supper was forgotten for a few minutes, as they hurried about to make the woman more comfortable. Susan, the youngest daughter, got a soup plate and eating utensils from a large pine cupboard and set another place at the table. "Don't forget a regular plate too," reminded her mother. Samuel tied a piece of stout cord from one chairback to another and Pamelia hung the wet stockings and shoes to dry.

She introduced herself to them, and after a few minutes of standing by the fire was more comfortable. Her feet were warm in the fleece lined slippers Alice had brought. In the meantime Pamelia ladled out the soup and they all went over to the sawbuck table. "You sit over there, where Susan has set a place for you, next to Mr. Finch," said Pamelia.

"It's good of you folks to take me in like this—make me feel so welcome," said the woman as she sat down and savored the steaming soup. "You won't be sorry either. No, you won't be sorry," she repeated.

Now just what does she mean? wondered Pamelia. Samuel asked the blessing and they began supper. Pamelia had baked bread that day and it was warm from the oven. She cut through the crispy crust, giving each one a piece. The home-churned butter melted into golden pools as they spread it over the thick slices.

There was more than potato soup. They had a ham from which Pamelia had carved several slices, some late squash and apple pie. And because they were still English by tradition, a steaming pot of tea was at Pamelia's place for the warm embracing drink it was.

During supper it was decided the woman would stay for the night. "You can't go out this time of night, in this weather. It's no bother for us to have you," said Pamelia with Samuel agreeing.

The woman gave an inward sigh of relief. It was now pitch dark outside and still storming. "I wish there was some way I could repay you," she said.

"Don't even think about repaying," said Pamelia.

It was obvious their guest was very hungry for she could scarcely join in any more conversation until she had gotten her fill. After a time she began to talk. "I'm a clairvoyant," she informed them, looking intently first at Samuel and then Pamelia. "If you wish, I can tell you what I see in the past and in your future."

This was the last thing the Finches would have anticipated. Samuel said, "We've never talked with a fortune teller, never been that interested in the occult. But it would be interesting to hear what you have to say." He looked toward his wife and received an approving, if somewhat hesitant nod.

After the dishes were washed and packed away and table cleared the woman asked for a pencil.

"Do you want a piece of paper too?" asked Pamelia.

"No, just the pencil will be enough," replied the clairvoyant.

Wondering what the woman wanted it for, Pamelia went to the table where they kept such things and took out a pencil. She handed it to the woman who walked over to the table and sat down. She took it in her left hand and made motions as if writing with some awkwardness. "This," she said, "was how the Reverend Johnathan Finch had to write after his service in the Revolutionary War. He received a wound to his right hand incapacitating the use of it."

This was well known to Johnathan Finch's descendants but the clairvoyant was a stranger to the area and to the family. They continued to listen in amazement as she told them of their grandfather's disability and about other members of the family. Especially interesting were things relating to themselves which had happened during previous years.

"You had a baby born to you but you waited too long to give it a name. Because of this he was taken from you by death. If you ever have another son you should name him after his father's mother who is no longer living."

Samuel and Pamelia sat in almost stunned silence as they looked at this small, wizened person before them. "My mother's maiden name was Betsy Clement," stated Samuel.

The clairvoyant emphasized again, if they ever had another baby boy and wanted it to live they should remember what she had said.

(When their next baby, a boy, was born they were afraid not to use the name and did so forthwith, naming him Henry Clement Finch.)

She continued to fascinate them with her stories

108

and predictions. Samuel had replaced wood twice on the fire but now, as it burned low again he said, "This has been a most unusual and enjoyable evening but I think we are all ready for bed."

The next morning the woman appeared rested and her countenance which had been so intense was now more relaxed. "I had a good night's sleep. I'm grateful; thank you again."

She departed after breakfast and the Finches never heard of, or saw her again. How much the name Clement ever had to do with their son's miraculous escapes no one knows. Some were hair breadth as one incident which happened during the winter when Clement was four years old. He and another boy were playing some distance from his house. A load of logs came by and they hitched a ride. The logs were being drawn from nearby Maxon Mountain to the frozen Sacandaga River. From there they would eventually float downstream during the spring run-off headed for the sawmill at Conklinville.

When the wagon reached its destination on the river it was unloaded. Clement and his friend had already jumped off and begun playing around the piles of logs. Some had been there for several days and lay on the ice in disarray, coated with a slippery crust. The boys ran to the top of one pile and slid down and then to another. They did this again and again. Upon reaching the foot of the last slide they came to a large mound of ice in the river. Clement thought it would make an ideal ride and climbed up on it. The minute he did, it capsized and he plunged into the frigid river, several feet over his head. The mound had proven to be an air hill with no ice under the crusted dome.

He grasped for the sides, calling for help. But the log team with their driver had returned to the mountain. His companion was so frightened at what had happened he ran for home leaving Clement alone. Soaked clothes dragging him down, he kept trying frantically for a good hold on the icy sides of the hole. But his fingers slipped each time as he tried to pull himself up. With a final effort he pressed his arms down on the ice around the hole and with all his strength pushed upward. This time he threw himself free and over onto a firm surface. He lay there for a minute or two then, getting to his feet, started for home about a mile away.

When he arrived his clothes were frozen stiff for it was an unusually cold day. His mother had gone to her father's birthday party, but his two sisters were still there. They stripped the frozen clothes from him and he put on his best suit. Except for chilly sensations alternated with hot flashes, he was ready to go to the party.

His grandfather was seventy-five years old and always made a practice on his birthday to jump into the air and strike his heels together twice before landing. He performed the feat that evening which was well remembered by Clement.

But almost everyone else there was thinking of the greater feat performed that day when a small boy emerged from the icy waters of the Sacandaga River.

See Appendix: The Clairvoyant.

A Calling

Recollections of Dr. Henry Clement Finch

"I lived at the Fish House until eight years old and my life was the usual one for a young boy of that age. I went fishing, climbed about my father's grist mill, swam in the mill pond and Sacandaga River and hiked through the nearby woods. Then my father sold the grist mill and bought a farm about one mile north of the Village of Broadalbin where we moved. There I worked on the farm in the summer months and attended school during the winter term. Owing to the depression during those five to ten years from 1879 on, farming was not profitable and money was very scarce.

"Notwithstanding the fact that I enjoyed farming, loved to plant and see things grow, the crops were in poor demand. I liked to work but it didn't bring in much cash and I began to think what I wanted to choose as a lifetime pursuit.

"Once when I was ill the doctor was sent for

and came to see me. I thought what a grand life it was, and what a satisfaction it was to treat the ill and give relief to the suffering. I decided I would like to become a doctor. But money was not plentiful and with the financial depression at that time my father was not able to help me much. It looked to him like a big proposition. To me, with the enthusiasm I had to become a physician, I felt I must carry it out. But father said, 'You stay with me here on the farm and we will pay up the mortgage. When I am through with the place it will be yours.'

"It looked like the best I could do under the circumstances and I continued to stay with him. But one day I was working all alone hoeing corn and potatoes in one of the back fields and began to think about it again. I thought I could never be contented to stay on a farm and hoe and dig all my life even if I had a dozen farms, when I might do the work of relieving the sick and suffering. There had to be some way.

"I told my father if he would give me seventy-five cents a day I would stay with him through the summers and do chores for my board during the winter. On Saturdays I would help thrash and chop wood. The proceeds would help pay my way through college. When he saw that I would not be satisfied to stay with him on the farm he said, 'Well, do as you think best and I will help you all I can.'

"So I worked and saved at seventy-five cents a day until I had enough to begin with. Through hard work during the summers, and strict economy I managed to get quite a start. With the help of my sister and father I borrowed enough to finish my education. I was then perfectly satisfied and contented.

"During my medical College course I had William J. Peddie as a roommate. We rented a room, bought our provisions and hired the young lady of the house to do our cooking. In that way we saved some on our expenses which was necessary to help both of us complete our course.

"I married a physician's daughter, Lottie Barker, and after graduation began the practice of medicine with my father-in-law, Dr. Barker, in Broadalbin, New York. I was active in practice in the same place for nearly fifty years."

The Lady With the Snake in Her

The third story told by Dr. Henry Clement Finch when he was a practicing physician residing in the Village of Broadalbin, New York, begins:

"In the year 1870 I was twelve years old. We lived on a farm near Broadalbin and each Saturday morning I was entrusted with going to the village grocery store to purchase supplies for the family. On one of these occasions I met a horse doctor who was relating a story to the group of men usually gathered near the back of the store swapping news and gossip with all who came in.

"The old horse doctor was telling a very exciting and unique story about his daughter, Martha. As I listened, I heard him say that five years ago, when his daughter was fourteen years old, she was lying down flat on her stomach drinking out of a boiling spring in the back lot and accidently swallowed a very tiny snake. It was his idea and belief that the snake was still in her stomach, and by this time it had grown to a considerable size because she could plainly feel the vermicular movements which often resulted in bringing on very severe convulsions and unconsciousness.

"I became so interested in the stories about his girl he was sure to tell to the large gathering at the grocery store in the most excited and demonstrative manner, that I looked forward each week to hearing all the new developments in the case.

"He told of all the doctors who had been called and their various diagnoses and treatment. It was before the days of the X-ray. In fact, doctors were not required to obtain a diploma before hanging out their shingle to practice medicine. It is amusing to recall the many conclusions, and resulting treatment to which the young girl submitted.

"By this time I had made myself known to the horse doctor and on one very important occasion he said to me, 'I think we are on the right track now. We have changed doctors, and located an old Indian doctor living some distance away.'

"After having tried nearly all the doctors and so-called doctors in the locality, and dosing her with all sorts and kinds of nostrums and concoctions for this period of five years, with no beneficial results, 'I think now,' he said, 'we have the right doctor who understands her case. He gave her a very strong dose which brought away the skin of the snake and he thinks the next one will bring the snake.'

"I can assure you I was on hand during his next visit to learn the results. But the next dose was never given. The old Indian doctor, who bore the name 'Rankey', rarely bathed or changed his clothes. His manner became so severe and taciturn during the treatment that the father was afraid this next dose would be too much and his daughter could not endure it. So fortunately it was never tried.

"During these years and the years that followed, she was bedridden. Her father had spent quite a fortune for medical care and treatment. Her mother had worn herself out and finally both parents passed on, largely as a result of the strenuous care they had given their beautiful daughter.

"Her teen-age lover, Billy, who had stood by her and a sister, Mary, were the only ones left to care for her.

"Time passed and from year to year I would hear of her as the freak of the community. People came from far and near to see the bedridden girl with a snake in her. On a Sunday afternoon, as had been the custom with her parents, Martha would be installed on the front piazza, and there people would view her, white and limpid, as they passed by in their carriages.

"I finished school, went to college and graduated from Albany Medical College in 1882. During all my medical course I was intensely interested in anything pertaining to worms or snakes in the human stomach or bowels, owing to the knowledge and interest of Martha's case. After graduation I settled in my home town and began the practice of medicine. Can you imagine my great curiosity and excitement when I was called to treat Martha, whom I had heard so much about and whose condition I had speculated on for twenty-five years?

"I was young, had only been practicing medicine a short time, when I had the call to treat this great mystery. But with the exhaustive study I had made of anything pertaining to living creatures in the human organs, I was ready for the proposition and looked forward with great interest and pleasure to making the most extended and exhaustive study of this case to determine, if possible, what the creature really was.

"Her twenty-five years in bed had been spent

mainly by telling people of her condition. She related cause and all the symptoms and treatment connected with her case. Her expression was usually resigned and passive, but during these times of recounting her face became animated, brown eyes intent and sparkling. No doubt she had told this over and over, thousands of times, until she had the story down pat and believed every word of it was true.

"When I arrived at her bedside she began her story and it was a long one too. But I listened very attentively. I was careful to put her through every physiological and pathological test known to the physician at that time, fifty years ago.

"I examined every organ in her body. I felt the snake (?) jump in her body, and listened to all her idiosyncracies, especially when under the influence of medicines and stimulants that might make the creature angry. She warned me that, whatever I did for her, I must be very careful not to make the snake mad. If I did she would not get a wink of sleep, and her very life would be in danger.

"I promised that I would do nothing to jeopardize her condition or make her worse.

"No doubt during all the strenuous treatments to which she had been subjected, her life had been put to the test and even laid low from the harsh remedies which had been employed without doing her a particle of good.

"She could always find the snake and feel him jump. Could I? Upon my first lengthy examination I found her suffering with a slight attack of the grippe. Again she cautioned me not to disturb the snake. I prescribed some simple remedies which would not stimulate the circulation very much for I knew if I did there would be commotion she would attribute to the snake's antics.

"I made her numerous visits and studied her case carefully for several days before I was ready to commit myself on a diagnosis. We had a few pleasant visits until I thought I had fully gained her confidence and also that of her sweetheart and sister. I then said to her, 'Martha, I think Billy has been waiting a long time for you, more than twenty-five years, and is wondering if you will ever be able to marry him. Do you think it is fair to keep him waiting longer? You know, your sister and several other young ladies are anxious to make him happy. Under the circumstances, don't you think you should release him from his promise?'

"With downcast expression her reply was, 'Can't you get this reptile away and cure me of such an affliction so our promises can be fulfilled? That's

what I called you for. I believe you can, can't you?
I can't give him up!"

"'Yes, I can, if you will promise to comply with
all my directions. You will have to follow every
detail and do exactly as I tell you.'

"'I'll do anything to get better!'

"'Very well, you begin by sitting up on the edge
of the bed for five minutes once or twice a day
until you can sit in a chair. Then you can lengthen
the time and begin to take a step or two. After
doing this for a little time you will begin to get
more strength and walk around the room like other
people and get well.'

"'Yes, but what about the snake? How will you
get him?'

"'Martha,' I said, 'you haven't any snake.'

"'Haven't any snake! What do you mean? Haven't
you felt it jumpin' and squirmin'; don't you think
I've told you the truth?'

"Just as I suspected, she was angry and became
rebellious. I tried to be as tactful as I could. But
when I insisted she had no snake in her she threw
a hysterical fit, turned her face to the wall and said,
'If I'd known you thought I didn't have a snake
I wouldn't have allowed you to give me one drop
of medicine. You might have made the snake mad

123

and killed me. You can never give me another drop of medicine!'

"Billy and Martha's sister tried to console her. They were afraid the snake would throw another fit. I told them not to worry and assured them there was no danger. But Martha was through with me. And as for taking medicine from me, that was entirely out of the question. But that didn't trouble me, it was a case that didn't need medicine. What she needed was a good heart to heart talk and explanation of her true condition.

"She had a clear case of hysteria from beginning to end. Instead of whimsical notions from a superstitious father, she should have been told the truth about her hysterical condition. This would have saved her twenty-five years of suffering and a fortune spent on her without help or relief.

"I explained to her the anatomy and physiological actions of the large aortic artery that ascends along the spinal column and the pulsation of this artery which she thought to be the jumps and squirms of the serpent. When she grew excited and nervous, its pulsations were harder. Following the effects of stimulating drugs and excitants, the pulsations increased, which she attributed to the actions of the snake. All this was very real to her.

124

"After rehearsing the story of drinking the snake, and all the notoriety she had received from telling the story to the thousands of people who had visited her as a living curiosity, it had so fixed itself upon her mind that she fully believed it was true. The snake was in her stomach, growing larger and larger each year, as she grew thinner and the artery more perceptible to the touch. And all its movements, which she thought were the antics of the snake, became more discernable.

"Although she was angry and said I made the snake madder, I told her the whole story of the diagnosis and prognosis of her case. Then I said if she would make the effort to get strong and well along the lines mapped out to her, she would be able to care for herself, relieving her sister whose health was now broken. Once again she would be able to get out in the sunshine and air and prevent tuberculosis.

"To prove that my approach was correct and that she did absorb what I said to her, it was only a short time before I heard she was up and about the house. Just about one year had passed since my last visit to her.

"She eventually married Billy who had waited so

long for her hand. It was some time after her marriage she was taken ill and sent for me.

"I didn't mention the snake to her, nor did she to me. But upon a thorough examination I discovered just what I had feared might happen from the confinement in bed so many years with lack of sunshine and fresh air. She had developed tuberculosis and was then in a serious stage of the disease.

"She lived and did her housework more than eight years after she married. She never again mentioned her years of confinement to me until just a few weeks before her death, when she fully appreciated her serious condition. She said to me, 'Doctor, will you make me a promise?'

"I said I certainly would if possible and she said, 'Will you have an autopsy on me when I'm gone and you'll find that I was right?'

"The idea had so impressed itself upon her mind and nervous system that she still thought she must have a snake.

"I carried out her wish and performed the autopsy. She had told all the neighbors what I had promised to do, and what I would find. So when I went to perform the autopsy and carry out my promise, the house was filled with curious spectators.

"I found nothing abnormal in her whole system,

126

except the lungs. They were almost entirely consumed by tuberculosis.''

Shoofly

The little village of Broadalbin, New York, is located between the larger settlements of Saratoga and Johnstown. It is much the same in appearance today as at the turn of the century. Old houses, surrounded by well-kept lawns and gardens, are set back from tree-shaded streets. Many years ago a few wealthy and illustrious families added a certain elegance of atmosphere which the place now misses. But even yet, the homes look sedately out at the world from unblinking eyes and tell of old glories.

Dr. Henry C. Finch and his wife, Lottie, lived on Main Street, close by the small village green. The doctor had been born in a log cabin not far from the village. During his exciting and eventful lifetime he was to be credited with helping start the first bank in the area, a power and light company, a drug store and one of the principal figures in a knitting company employing several hundred people.

129

During all this activity, he was on call around the clock as a physician. But before he attained this position of real importance among the people in the county and state, he and his wife experienced all the uncertainties and lean years of most young, struggling doctors. Lottie, daughter of a country doctor, was an excellent helpmate and her abiding sense of humor was to stand the family in good stead more than once.

"We have an invitation from the Robert Chambers'" said Mrs. Finch, drying her hands on her apron as she hurried into the doctor's office. "Next Friday afternoon at two-thirty," she continued, placing the invitation on the doctor's desk in front of him.

Robert Chambers was one of the most eminent men living at Broadalbin. He had already attained nation-wide attention for the books he had written and was to continue to be popular with such stories as *Cardigan* and *Little Red Foot*. His new home, just completed, was the largest in the village. It was handsome and imposing, with tall white-fluted columns stretching across the front portico. The house had been furnished with beautiful and rare furniture, paintings, and bric-a-brac. The time had now arrived to invite certain of the townspeople to a house warming. A selective list was drawn up and invitations sent out. One of these invitations was delivered by coachman to the home of Dr. and Mrs. Finch. News of events travels rapidly in a small village, and Mrs. Finch already knew about the coming party. Even the handyman filled her in on many of the details. However, she hadn't been sure about the exact day and time. This was important because she had just one suitable dress, the white crochet, which she would have to get ready. It wouldn't do even to think of going into Johnstown or Amsterdam to buy a new one. The doctor had just purchased some office equipment and the family till was at a low ebb. She could iron out the pink ribbon sash to wear with the dress.

The night before the party, Mrs. Finch worked in the kitchen until late. Particular pains had to be taken with the starching solution of sugar and water so the dress would be brought to just the right, attractive crispness. Her irons on the stove couldn't be allowed to get too hot or they would scorch the material. It was almost midnight before she finished and held the dress up to admire. It did look nice.

My, it's warm, she thought, pushing the damp hair back from her forehead. Hadn't cooled off much during the evening.

Friday turned out to be one of those steaming August days with the sun burning through the morning haze. "Nice day for the Chambers' party, but it's a hot one," exclaimed the doctor, mopping his brow with a handkerchief as he came into the kitchen from the office. Mrs. Lee and her son had just left. The boy was the first patient that day. He had obviously contracted the measles, and the doctor ordered him home and to bed. Never can tell about the damage measles will do, he reflected.

Mrs. Finch waited until it was almost time to leave for the party before slipping into the crisp lace dress, and the doctor helped her tie the big pink sash around her waist. "Pretty as a picture," he said, stepping back to admire his wife.

When they walked out of the house, the heat hit them with almost breathtaking intensity. "It's the warmest day we've had this summer," commented Mrs. Finch.

"You look as cool as a cucumber in that dress," said the doctor, helping his wife into the carriage and taking his place beside her.

They were soon at the Chambers' house, in the huge entrance hall, being greeted by Mr. and Mrs. Robert Chambers. It was exciting thought Mrs.

Finch, looking about and recognizing some of the other guests.

Even with the gaiety and animation of the party, the heat was terribly oppressing. Mrs. Finch knew it was surely readying for a thunder storm. And something had begun to annoy her. The dress, once so stiffly starched, had started to wilt! And even worse, it seemed that every fly in the mansion was alighting upon her. They were unreasonably persistent and refused to go away when she brushed them off. Every time the doors were opened for guests to come and go, more flies found their way to the dress starched with sugar. Each new fly caused her additional embarrassment. She just had to leave and made her way over to the doctor, who was talking with a group of men. When he saw her approach, he knew something was wrong and excused himself.

"We've got to leave," she whispered up at him.

"It's quite early to be leaving," replied the doctor as he flicked a fly from his wife's shoulder.

She almost cried, "That's why we must go. It's the flies and the dress!"

The doctor looked at her, puzzled for a moment. "I don't understand," he said.

She grasped his hand and almost dragged him

toward the hall. "I'll explain when we are outside," she said.

They walked over to Mr. and Mrs. Chambers. "You have a lovely home. Thanks so much for inviting us to see it. Sorry we have to go now, but the doctor has some calls to make that just can't wait," said Mrs. Finch.

Mr. and Mrs. Chambers went through the formalities of shaking hands again as Mr. Chambers watched a fly, large as a button, crawl along Mrs. Finch's white dress, while three or four others buzzed around her shoulders. "Come again soon," said Mrs. Chambers.

When they were outside the large house, Mrs. Finch told her husband what had happened. By now she had regained her composure. "The next time I wear this dress, instead of a satin sash I'll use a bow of flypaper!"

See Appendix: Shoofly.

Appendix

The Story of Bull Run

For those of you who don't know the location of Bull Run in Fulton County here in New York State, the following directions will get you there. Travel north on Bleecker Street which originates on West Fulton Street in Gloversville, until you come to the intersection of Bleecker Street and West 11th Avenue. Turn left at this four corners known years ago, some say, as Cape Horn because of a promontory, part of which is still visible, and proceed on route 309. You will come to the next four corners where West State Street Extension intercepts route 309. Keep going to the next four corners where Phelps Street Extension intercepts and proceed on route 309 to the foot of Bleecker Mountain. You have now reached Bull Run where the Bulls

135

lived. There are a few homes here and a small, old cut stone bridge spanning a creek.

The lady who told me this story was, as I remember, related to the early settlers of this region.

Pitch, the card game referred to in the story, was often an evening's or rainy afternoon's pastime and is still played in Adirondack country.

The Dominie

I have corresponded with Mrs. Marjorie M. Clemans whose deceased husband, the Reverend H. Clemans, was a grandson of Dominie Clemans. The grandson was a minister for several years in New York City. Mrs. Clemans wrote the following in answer to my querry about the Dominie.

"From all accounts Dominie Clemans was quite a character. He died before my husband was born— in fact he was nine years younger than Abraham Lincoln. If there was any kinship between him and Samuel L. Clemens it must have been remote. However, the story is that he changed the spelling of his name to Clemans because he disagreed with some of Mark Twain's attitudes concerning the Civil War.

"Mark Twain's aunt, Mrs. Shaw, lived in Manhattan during her later years and my husband called on her regularly. She always laughed and complimented him on the fact he was the only one she ever knew of that name who didn't claim near kinship.

"Dominie Clemans was Chaplain of the 115th N.Y. Volunteers—the Iron Hearted Regiment—under Colonel Sammons and raised by him (Sammons). They furnished their own horses and much of their food. I remember seeing a letter written to Chaplain Clemans from a merchant in New York who took charge of transporting the latter's (Clemans') horse across town to a boat for shipment. There was some expense involved and the chaplain felt the price was exorbitant and said so. The gist of the Merchant's reply was, "Dammit, I don't care if you are a preacher, you drive a hard bargain."

I am indebted to the late William H. Cunning for the story about Dominie Clemans. Mr. Cunning was a native of the Broadalbin area and lived there until adulthood. He later moved to Akron, Ohio. Upon retirement from a position with one of the rubber manufacturing companies, he returned to Fulton County and lived in Gloversville, N. Y.

Nickname

The old grist mill referred to in the story is still standing at Vail Mills. It used to be called Vail's Mills[1] by many, including the eminent historian, Washington Frothingham, in his book, *The History of Fulton County, New York.* The brick structure was converted into a restaurant. Occupants change from time to time so at this writing some other enterprise may occupy the premises. The pond which was located across the road from the grist mill was drained and just the basin remains, now filled with weeds.

Munsonville[2] which was named after Ebenezer Munson,[3] no longer exists and much of the land it occupied is now under the waters of Great Sacandaga Lake. The settlement was located near what is now

---

1. Frothingham, Washington, *History of Fulton County, New York,* Pub. D. Mason & Co. 1892, p. 523.
2. *Ibid.* 523.
3. *Ibid.* 524.

138

called Van Denburgh's Point. Mr. Munson married a Van Denburgh. He eventually became a manufacturer of wagon wheels and the business was located at Munsonville.

Ebenezer lived on into his nineties and is buried in the Broadalbin Cemetery not far from author Robert W. Chambers' plot.

If one has further interest in identifying various woods by their aroma, reference can be found in: *What Wood Is That? A Manual of Wood Identification* by Edlin, Herbert L., published 1969; Viking Press, page 70; chapter entitled: Smells.

Mr. Lester Burgess tells me that in the early nineteen hundreds he worked for Charlie Vail at Vail Mills. At that time, he says, the hamlet consisted of a few houses, a saw mill, box shop, grist mill and a Mr. Vosburgh operated a general store.

It was in the box manufacturing phase of the Vail enterprises that Mr. Burgess was employed as driver of a team of horses. The box shop was located over the saw mill and here various size wooden cases were constructed. Mr. Burgess said he reported for work at 7 A.M. when the boxes were loaded on his wagon, often for delivery to the Morris Mills, a knit goods mill in Amsterdam, New York.

Peggy Tight Hole

The epilogue to this story is not a happy one. It was told to me by a native of the area, now in his 90's.

In the matter of a few weeks the entire community took up the name Peggy Tight Hole. People were fascinated by its originality and application to this older man who, though not a buffoon, was susceptible to the calls and gibes of the youths as he walked about town. After a time he became so sensitive to hearing himself referred to as Peggy Tight Hole, or sometimes just Peggy that, red faced with emotion, he would turn and spit out oaths at his tantalizers.

This made things worse. As time passed the general populace realized he was growing strange, muttering to himself as he walked along the streets. He was no longer friendly with his neighbors and cut himself off from his usual day to day contacts. But for his wife, some even thought he should be "put away." Nothing was done about this until one day a bizarre incident took place.

In the west end of the village stood a magnificent mansion on the corner of West Fulton Street and

North McNab Avenue. The house was occupied by the McNab[1] family. They had a small chicken house on the grounds and on this particular day he (Peggy Tight Hole) was walking past the house and a rooster began to crow. What he heard was not the lusty crowing of the cock but the taunting words, PEGGY TIGHT HOLE.

All the rage contained so long in him without manifesting itself in actual violence now broke loose. He raced across the lawn toward the rear of the property until he reached the chicken yard. As he threw open the gate the rooster crowed again. Now, completely berserk, he lunged for the bird, chasing it around and around the enclosure. Great commotion ensued and aroused the McNabs. But too late—he had already caught the rooster and wrung its neck.

The McNabs were people to be reckoned with. While many citizens thought something should be done for this troubled man, he continued to walk the streets listening to a name he had grown to despise. Perhaps, unknowingly, a certain sadistic

---

1. Frothinghan, Washington, *History of Fulton County, N.Y.* D. Mason and Company, 1892, pp. 172–176.
Ibid: p. 278.
Ibid: (Family Sketches) p. 88.

pleasure resulted for some as they watched him teased to the point of insanity. In any event, after the attack on the McNab rooster it wasn't long before, with his wife's consent, he was committed to an asylum.

He was away, we don't know how long, but eventually released and returned home. It is assumed by this time other happenings in the community had replaced his in prominence and he was able to cope, for the story ends and we hear no more accounts of Peggy Tight Hole.

The McNab mansion was razed several years ago and the site is now occupied by McNab Elementary School.

A Church From Devil's Money

Helen Martin Strong related this story to me as it was told to her by Mr. and Mrs. Kennedy of Johnstown, New York. For those of you who don't know—Mrs. Strong, along with the Naylor family, were owners of Gloversville's largest department store. It was called Martin & Naylor's.

The Kennedys, on their way to the Saratoga Spa

horse races one day in August, stopped at the department store. Upon seeing their friend, Mrs. Strong, they visited for a few minutes and told her the story.

After hearing the folktale from Mrs. Strong I was interested in learning more about it. I visited Perth and interviewed a family which had lived there many years. They mentioned I might talk with the McQueens, another early settler. This led me to a spokesman for the family, Harold H. McQueen of South Pasadena, California, who wrote:

"I never heard it before (a church from devil's money) and I strongly suspect that it may have been a tradition attached to some other church in the general area and in the course of many verbal tellings may have been wrongly identified with the Perth church. The church in Perth was completed in 1831, the brick being furnished by James Stewart."

May 29, 1982 there was a copy of an early photograph in a local Sunday newspaper of the old United Presbyterian Church as it appeared about 1909. The caption related a tornado went through Perth in 1918 which did considerable damage to the church, tearing off the roof, smashing windows and shutters and cracking the bell tower.

Indian at the Window

My grandmother, Elizabeth Dennie Abbey, told me this story which had been related to her when a young girl, growing up near Mayfield, New York in a small hamlet called Dennie Hollow.

The Dennies[1] settled the area prior to the American Revolution and stories of events which often included Indians were not uncommon and often told and retold from one generation to the next.

Dennie Hollow is located about two miles from the village of Mayfield. As one proceeds northward on New York State highway route 30, a marker, Dennie Road, can be seen from the highway. A few of the old houses remain from earlier days mixed with others of a more recent vintage.

For the first white settlers, farming was the order of the day. Then, in the mid 1800's, lime deposits were explored on the Dennie lands. Kilns were built and for several years lime[2] was sold locally and also hauled by horse and wagon from Dennie Hollow to the railroad station at Fonda, New York, where it was shipped to industries outside the area.

---

1. Frothingham, Washington, *History of Fulton County, New York,* D. Mason pub. p. 509.
2. *Ibid.* p. 508.

144

The Amah's Prayer

Jack's Ready to Wear Shop, proprietor Jacob Gurowitz, which was located at 201 North Main Street in Gloversville is now gone. The old, two story wood frame building which housed the business was demolished several years ago and replaced by a concrete block one story building where pizza, Italian bread, and other items are sold. For over twenty years my real estate office was located at 211 North Main Street, a close neighbor to my good friend Jack.

Though *The Amah's Prayer* takes us to a distant locale it belongs here, where told; therefore, I have included it among these folk stories.

The Unfortunate Pig

As veins in a leaf, country roads and narrow lanes once coursed their way through our Yorker countryside. Main roads branched off into smaller dirt ones and the smaller roads off into dead end obscurity. Often these less traveled routes led to an

145

early settler's home. The old, forgotten roads neglected and washed out in many places, are not traversable by automobile. Now, in wintertime, they provide excellent trails for cross-country skiers.

A caved in foundation wall, camouflaged by brush and leaves, hidden from the casual observer, is often all that remains of a domicile. Old apple trees and lilacs gone wild, unwilling to give up, stay on to tell of better days. Sometimes a small, neglected family cemetery with its ancient headstones give clues as to who lived in the area.

The little farm where the lady resided who had the pig was located alongside one of these lesser traveled roads. According to the teller of the story it was not far from Skunk Hollow in Fulton County, and Bull Run was just over the hill and through a dale.

We searched for the farmhouse and could find no trace of it. We concluded the building no longer existed. Perhaps it fell into disrepair and eventually capsized into its own cellar or burned to the ground to be numbered among those long forgotten homesteads which sheltered so many of our pioneering families. We will continue, my friend and I, to look and hopefully find the place where the house stood.

Once Upon a Time

(An Informative Letter)

An aura of dignified elegance was prevalent when the Husteds and other members of their family lived on Maple Street in the Village of Broadalbin, New York. Their homes were large with the servants to care for them. It was before the days of heavy federal taxes, and the pace was slower, allowing time to savor the good things of life.

Across from Colonel Husted's[1] home was a pond, idylic and resplendent with a golden swan boat to ply his family and summer visitors over its mirrored surface. One can only imagine a warm sunny day those many years ago with the Husteds and their guests enjoying the pastoral pleasures of this lovely place. A dam no longer retains the pond's waters and now, in summer, it is filled with a slumbering verdancy.

Miss M. K. (Kitty) Husted[2] was apparently a most delightful individual and beloved by those who

---

1. Frothingham, Washington, *History of Fulton County, New York*, pub. D. Mason and Company, 1892, p. 503.
2. *Ibid.* p. 503.

knew her. She and her family had the railroad station in the village constructed to resemble a Grecian edifice, complete with classic columns. Certainly an unexpected site for those summer guests who arrived by train at this little village in the Adirondack foothills.

A Broadalbin Free Reading Room for the villagers was endowed in memory of Colonel William H. Husted by Miss M. K. Husted, Mrs. Cromwell, Mrs. Beers and Charles and Seymour Husted.[3]

A few notes about the people and places mentioned in the letter in addition to those listed above:

Mrs. Chambers was the wife of Robert W. Chambers, the author.

The Duveen family were famous international art dealers.[4]

"On-A-Knoll" refers to an impressive home, located between Broadalbin and Vail Mills. It was first occupied by the Wards; then Dr. and Mrs. Percy Finch; to be followed by other occupants.

The Beers house, which Jim designates as once

3. *Ibid.* p. 82.
4. Behram, S. H., *Duveen,* pub. Random House, Inc. 1951.

belonging to his grandfather, Samuel Thompson, is a brick mansion located on Maple Street in Broadalbin.

The Littlejohns[5] mentioned in the letter came to Broadalbin from New York City and a son of theirs was born in Broadalbin, Fitz Hugh Littlejohn, who later was an attorney in the village. His maternal great grandfather was the French Count Larchar[6] who fought in the war of the Revolution.

The Cromwell twins, Gladys Louise Husted Cromwell and Dorothea Katherine Cromwell were prominent young women of their time.[7]

The Clairvoyant

This story is based on mention of a clairvoyant among the papers given to me by Cecile Hapeman

5. Frothingham, Washington, *History of Fulton County, New York,* pub. D. Mason and Company, 1892, p. 82.

6. *Ibid.* p. 82.

7. *The New York Times,* January 25, 1919, p. 1; January 26, 1919, p. 1; May 9, 1919, p. 20; October 7, 1919, p. 20; *New York Herald,* January 25, 1919, p. 1; *The Sun,* January 25, 1919, p. 1; *The Morning Herald,* January 25, 1919, p. 1, (Gloversville, N. Y.).

Clockson. Her mother, Grace Finch Hapeman, had an interest in history and folklore and saved certain material which interested her. I am not sure if this particular accounting of a clairvoyant, included in a brief biographical sketch, was penned by Dr. Henry Clement Finch[1] or his daughter, Grace. It is related in first person and then changes later to third person. I also remember the same story as told orally by other members of the family.

The doctor's mother, Pamelia Shew Finch, was a descendant of Godfrey Shew[2], veteran of the French and Indian Wars and the American Revolution. He was the first permanent white settler at Fish House and his son, Godfrey, was the first white child to be born there.

Dr. H. C. Finch graduated from Albany Medical

1. *Hudson-Mohawk Genealogical and Family Memoirs,* Lewis Historical Publishing Co., 1911, Vol. IV, pp. 153–154.

Today's Health: article "When Doctors Were Guinea Pigs" by Howard Earle, June 1962, pp. 50–53, pub. American Medical Association. (This article concerns an historic race between two doctors: the father, Henry Clement Finch in his horse and buggy and his son, Percy, racing in that new contraption— the automobile).

2. Simms, J. R., *Trappers of New York,* pub. 1846, pp. 21, 22, 25, 42, 43, 45, 50, 51, 54.

History of Montgomery and Fulton Counties, pub. 1878; F. W. Beers & Co., p. 232.

Sawyer, Donald J., *They Came to Sacandaga, The Story of Godfrey Shew: Fish House Patriot,* 1976; Prospect Books.

College and returned to the Broadalbin area where he practiced medicine for many years. He married a country doctor's daughter, Charlotte Barker. His patients included people living in and around the village countryside. Broadalbin attracted a few wealthy families from the New York City area who were also patients of Dr. Finch. Among these summer residents were Robert W. Chambers, the author, and also the Husteds. The latter family occupied the large home which included beautiful grounds called by many the Italian Gardens.

Shoofly

The old Finch home is still located on North Main Street in Broadalbin. Dr. H. C. Finch had his office here for many years and his son, Dr. Percy Finch, was also located here until moving to Gloversville. Later the house was occupied by Mr. and Mrs. Cecil Finch, a son of Dr. H. C. Finch. The house was eventually sold to someone outside the family.

Robert W. Chambers (1865–1933) was the author of several books and recognized during his prolific years as one of this country's outstanding writers. He is especially remembered in the Mohawk Valley and Adirondack region for his historical novels about these areas. Among these books are: *The Reckoning, Cardigan* and *The Little Red Foot.* He and his wife had a palatial home in Broadalbin which is referred to in Shoofly. It is located on the corner of North Main and North Streets and occupied at the present time by a religious order.

This story was told to me by Millicent Finch Chaloner, a daughter of Dr. and Mrs. H. C. Finch.